HEAD FIRST

The Language of the Head Voice:
A Concise Study of Learning to Sing
in the Head Voice

Denes Striny

Foreword by Birgit Nilsson

Hamilton Books
A member of
The Rowman & Littlefield Publishing Group
Lanham · Boulder · New York · Toronto · Plymouth, UK

Hamilton Books
4501 Forbes Boulevard
Suite 200
Lanham, Maryland 20706
Hamilton Books Acquisitions Department (301) 459-3366

Estover Road
Plymouth PL6 7PY
United Kingdom

Printed in the United States of America
British Library Cataloging in Publication Information Available

Library of Congress Control Number: 2006939831
ISBN-13: 978-0-7618-3671-1 (paperback : alk. paper)
ISBN-10: 0-7618-3671-3 (paperback : alk. paper)

∞™ The paper used in this publication meets the minimum requirements of American National Standard for Information Sciences—Permanence of Paper for Printed Library Materials, ANSI Z39.48—1984

Dedication
In Remembrance

On the morning of January 6th at my apartment in New York City, I had just finished a phone conversation with my editor Bruce Burch about my book *Head First: The Language of the Head Voice*. We both felt the book was nearing completion as we discussed the front and back cover. I had received, four days earlier, the finished digital picture that I wanted for the front cover. I had found that picture at the Metropolitan Opera Guild Office who gave permission for its use and formatted the picture for the dimensions of the revised book. The picture was that of Birgit Nilsson and Franco Corelli in a 1967 production of *Turandot*, a performance I attended while still in college. She had on that incredible head dress; the picture had it all.

I remember my first image of Birgit Nilsson while in high school from an old *Ed Sullivan Show*. She sang "*In questa reggia*" from Act II of *Turandot*. I had never heard an opera at this time and sat before the old black and white TV set stunned by the sound that she made with her voice—it was huge, exciting, beautiful, and bewildering. How did she do this? She was wearing a white, maybe taffeta dress, tightly fitted, and was standing in front of a trellis filled with roses. If there were any tension in her body one certainly would have seen it; but there was none. I didn't know anything about what I had just seen, but at that moment I knew I wanted to be a part of it. I followed Birgit's performances from the 60's to the end of her career.

In 1987, after a 17 performance run of *Die Meistersinger von Nürnberg* in Great Britain, singing my first Wagnerian role—Walther—I received a phone call from my best friend Michael Cordovana at The Catholic University of America in Washington, DC. Mike asked me if I would like to sing for Birgit Nilsson; he was bringing her to the university for a Master Class. I, of course, said "yes," it was a chance to meet and sing for the woman who had such a profound influence on me.

A month later I was in DC and had my first private lesson with her. There was another bond I had with Birgit. Only three weeks earlier I discovered through Catholic Charities in St. Paul, Minnesota (I'm an adopted kid) that my heritage was not German/Austrian, as I for many years had been told, but Swedish—on both sides. So when I met the great Birgit Nilsson for the first time, I felt that we had known each other forever. She responded quite personably. We laughed, joked, and kidded with each other and made some wonderful music for three days during that Master Class. She invited me to come to Buckaburg, Germany, that October where she was giving a month-long series of classes. I worked with her again privately and within the classes—often six hours a day, six days a week. We'd have breakfast together each morning and many times dinner; she wanted to teach me how to be Swedish, although she would tell me she thought there was a touch of Finnish in me, also.

This time with her was like a dream. We would work on German together in the evenings until she told me that I finally was speaking *Hoch Deutsch*. The main point that characterized our sessions was laughter, jokes, and mutual respect. We both had a tremendous respect for each other. Her knowledge and insight were unparalleled.

One morning after singing at a party given by the Count at the castle where we were staying (along with 600 of his closest friends), I arrived at breakfast to work with Birgit as usual, but she said frantically to me, "You do not have time to have breakfast; you have a lot of driving to do to get to Bayreuth by tomorrow morning. I spoke to Wieland last night and he wants to hear you tomorrow!" She had personally arranged for a private audition at the *Festspiele Haus* with one of the great Wagnerian directors.

I was thrilled; I was ecstatic; this really was a dream! Walking into the *Festspiele Haus*, I was told to report to the Bursar's Office to get my check; I had no idea what they were talking about and only later understood they were paying **me** to sing an audition. I was still awe-struck as I stood center stage with the set of *Siegfried* behind me, one light shining down front center with only Wolfgang Wagner as the audience in the auditorium. He wanted to hear the complete role of Siegmund from *Die Walküre*. What fun! What excitement! That was a moment I'll never forget. I owe that experience and many more to Birgit Nilsson.

For the next two years I worked with Birgit whenever she came to New York City; she would always give me a call when she came into town. I remember one call from her in 1993. She was coming to town to do a Master Class and also to participate in a 350th celebration of the Swedes landing in America. She asked if I would drive her down to the festivities—a big dinner with the King and Queen of Sweden at the Hotel Dupont in Wilmington, Delaware, and be her escort for the event.

We drove down; as Birgit would say, "What a hoot!" At 1 o'clock in the morning we left to return to New York City, laughing and talking non-stop. Suddenly I noticed we were surrounded by cornfields and complete darkness; I had confused the Jersey Turnpike with Interstate 95, and we were quite lost. There were no gas stations, no houses, and no lights. I couldn't believe it—lost in a cornfield with Birgit Nilsson! We had to drive around quite awhile before finding someone who could get us back on the path to New York City. We didn't really mind; we were able to enjoy the dilemma together, and it deepened our friendship and respect.

In 2001 I founded and was the Artistic Director for Shaker Mountain Opera at the Koussevitsky Arts Center in Pittsfield, Massachusetts. Birgit consented to be the Honorary Chair of the Festival. We opened with an amazing performance of *Die Walküre* which I conducted with the Albany Symphony Orchestra. The following year we went on to perform *Götterdämmerung*. All of this was inspired by this amazing friend and incredible force of nature. I'd send her tapes of all the performances and would always receive a very gracious response with a critique.

I hadn't intended these personal stories to appear in this book, but on that morning of January 6, 2006, something else happened. I heard that Birgit Nilsson had died. It is very hard to envision a world without Birgit. Her friendship gave me the strength to realize whatever potential exists in me. The battles she had with her voice as a beginning singer and with her early career showed me what kind of person it takes to accomplish "this thing" called music on a high level. I will always remember Birgit and will always be deeply indebted to her.

I've decided also to scatter some memorabilia of Birgit throughout the book because our mutual understanding and corroboration of this phenomenon called the Head Voice permeated both our lives. I came to her with my knowledge, understanding, and talent, but needed to hear "Yes, go for it." Birgit provided the approval which gave me confidence. The hours we spent at the keyboard where she would pick out an exercise on the piano, making up some words on the spot to go with the notes, and vocalize me while drinking coffee and eating pastries in a castle in Germany are unforgettable.

Denes Striny
New York, NY
January 2006

Contents

Forward: A Letter from Birgit Nilsson xi
Preface xiii
Acknowledgments xv
Introduction: Singers and How They Get That Way xvii

Part I: Choices
1. Head Voice and Chest Voice: *Registers and Voices* 3
2. Breathing—No Big Deal 13
3. All the Stuff You Want: *Pitch, Text, Musicality, Carrying Power* 23
4. Everyday Voices: *Speaking, Shouting, Belting, and Vocal Self-Image* 37
5. Vocal Constriction and Health 41

Part II: Getting There
6. *Bel Canto* and Head Voice: *What Happened?* 55
7. The *Passaggio*: *From What? To What?* 59
8. Finding a Voice 65
9. About Teachers 71
10. Getting In the Zone 85
11. In the Final Analysis, Do You Deserve It? 89
12. The Learning Process and the Exercises 95

Exercises 107
Appendix 113
Index 145

The illustrations on pages xii, 12, 40, and 106 were drawn by Jose Manuel Sossa.

COMPANION CD FOR THE BOOK
HEAD-FIRST: The Language of the Head Voice

The Evolution of Denes Striny's Voice: 18 years old to present

Track		
1.	Aria from *La Perichole* (18 years old; the next year my voice teacher had me singing baritone), 1964	2:57
2.	Grieg Song (Five years later as a bass-baritone), 1969	2:31
3.	Grieg Song (Same period), 1970	2:10
4.	Ravel Song (One year later), 1970	1:37
5.	Aria from *La Boheme* (One year later reworking myself with Music-Minus-One), 1971	4:07
6.	*Ariadne auf Naxos* (One year later, still by myself), 1971	:55
7.	*Saint of Bleecker Street* (Break in tape; still by myself singing with Wolf Trap Co., after which I moved to New York City), 1974	3:15
8.	*Madama Butterfly* (Still no teacher; one year later in New York, singing with Dallas Opera, Washington Opera, Providence Opera, Goldovsky Opera, and many concerts), 1975	1:23
9.	*Madama Butterfly* (New teacher now for five years, no quality left in voice, Washington, DC), 1981	1:10
10.	*Don Carlo* Aria (Carlo Bergonzi, Eugene Kohn, Piano) **This was the turning point**. I realized that I could not sing [u] and [o] and that this affected my complete voice and complete vocal technique, 1983	9:15
11.	*La Fanciulla del West* Excerpts in performance (after reworking one year by myself), 1984	8:19
12.	*Die Meistersinger von Nürnberg* Coaching with Birgit Nilsson (Germany; taped for Swedish TV), 1985	3:15
13.	*Die Walküre* Coaching with Birgit Nilsson (Germany; for Swedish TV), 1985	12:42
14.	*Wintersturmme* Party honoring Birgit in Germany, 1985	3:12
15.	*Die Meistersinger von Nürnberg* in performance (Leeds, Great Britain), 1986	4:57
16.	*Norma* Aria in performance (St. Paul, MN), 1991	5:05
17.	*Otello* Aria in concert (New York City), 1992	:55
18.	*Turandot* Aria in concert, 1992	2:37

[This was the end of the battle for me. I was tired of fighting my own voice, and felt that over the 28 tears I had made a pretty good stab at it. I sang with many great singers and conductors (Miriam Gauci, Maria Ewing, Justino Diaz, Malcolm Smith, Martina Arroyo, Leyla Gencer, Beverly Sills, Tatiana Troyanos, Antonio Ordonez, Yoko Watanabe, Debra Riedel, Sarah Brightman, George Manahan, Mstislav Rostropovich, Nicola Rescigno, Jacque Dellacote, and many others). I was very proud of what I had accomplished, but it could have been more fun along the way.]

HEAD FIRST:
The Language of the Head Voice

Companion Compact Disc
Musical examples of Denes Striny's evolving life as an international operatic tenor, as well as his work with Birgit Nilsson

"The book and the CD are remarkable!"
Christa Ludwig

Please send me the companion CD to Head First: ***The Language of the Head Voice***

Quantity ________ @ $11.95 = ________

$2.00 Shipping/Handling = ________

Sales Tax *(where applicable)* = ________

Total Enclosed = ________

~ Payment Method ~

___ Check or Money Order payable to: **Denes Striny**

___ Major Credit Card *(check card type and fill out account information)*

___ American Express ___ Visa ___ MasterCard

Account No. ____________________________________ Exp.Date _________

Signature ____

Name *(Print)* ____

Address ____

City ______________________________ State __________ Zip __________

Mailing Address: Denes Striny, PO Box 498, Canaan, NY 12029
CD is also available online at: **www.DenesStriny.com**
Please allow 4 – 6 weeks for delivery

Foreword
A Letter from Birgit Nilsson

July 4, 1996

Dear Denes,

Wow! I must say that you have done a fabulous job, and I am full of admiration. You also seem to be a first class physician. Where have you learned everything?

As I mentioned to you earlier, I don't feel my English is good enough to write a complete chapter for your book. But I do have a few things to say. Ha!

As you know, I always speak about the two pools: the high placement in the forehead, and the low support. Some come by the feeling of low support when they get an idea of high placement of tone. For it is then that everything falls into the right place: the larynx, the pharynx, the tongue, etc. The **vocal cords will be released from the press**, and at that point the tone gets another dimension, much more beautiful, because then **our whole body becomes the instrument**.

Singing in this way is like a fountain with a plastic ball on the top which floats wonderfully on the water stream. **The body should nowhere be hard or constricted but elastic**. It takes time to develop this. For me it took almost ten years to relax my overworked vocal cords. Therefore, the sooner a student learns how the body is functioning, the better!

As you write in your book: "Great singers usually talk only about breath, because that is all they feel." This is exactly why they **are** great singers.

Continued success with your teaching and your book. I think it is a great work. Take care and much love.

Fondly,
Birgit

Preface

It is not possible to write about vocal history in a vacuum. No matter how much teachers and students of voice may wish to avoid contaminating their understanding of the past with new values in the present, they cannot ignore the fact that both writer and reader are inevitably affected by the assumptions and beliefs that have been passed down. Many of the issues addressed in this book as problems are viewed today as "givens," not to be rethought. It would be impossible to present a persuasive argument for the significance of such issues without examining, at some length, the genesis of the issues and the widespread preconceptions regarding causations.

The mission of this book is two-fold. Firstly, to engage the reader in a new way of thinking whereby one starts to realize that the sound of a singing or speaking voice has to do with how one uses his or her voice. HOW one speaks or sings. The accompanying CD of the Author's voice shows that when you change the way that you sing—you change the sound that you sing. **Cause and Effect!** Leontyne Price, Robert Merrill, Christa Ludwig, Nicolai Ghiarov, Rene Pape, Franco Corelli, Joan Sutherland, Ruth Ann Swenson, and Luciano Pavarotti all sing in a certain way, creating a certain sound. We, as listeners, tend to compartmentalize this achievement in a category called "Of course it's great singing—it's Leontyne, Birgit, Jussi. . . ." So now we the listeners don't have to feel bad about not being able to create this same kind of sound. "God just didn't give me the voice" should be changed to "I wish I sang in the way that Leontyne sings!"

The second half of the mission is to be as concise as possible in explaining "TEXTURE." Texture is the sound that is fed by breath to convey the voice. We all have many textures we can use. Some textures are open, some are tight, and some almost closed (causing the battle with the breath because the respiratory system is in a fight to stay open). However, there is one texture, and only one, that is completely open, therefore, totally free. This is the texture of great singing—not good or real good, *but great!* It is the texture that does not tighten the valve (larynx) and cause closure and a muscular battle with the breath. This "great singer" texture is very specific because it bypasses overt muscular involvement and is seemingly an "out of body experience" for the doer. This phenomenon cannot be explained to anyone who has not experienced it. In discussing this topic, we have a terminology problem. The words mean different things to people who have not had the experience. When great singers tell us what they feel when they sing, they are telling us the whole story. We however, only can grasp it to the degree that we can do it (sing in that way). **Cause and Effect.** If we do not sing in that way, we can not feel those sensations and, therefore, we cannot make those sounds.

This book will lead singers into a new way of listening, learning, doing, feeling, and sounding. It is a wonderful journey to take and will assist them in finding their "Total Vocal Potential." They will own it; they will understand it; but, unfortunately, they will not be able to converse on any real level with others who do not sing in this way. So, when asked, "How do you make that sound?" you too will say, "It was a gift from God. I don't know why He chose me, but I am glad that He did."

Acknowledgements

I wish to thank several people who were instrumental in this book being written. Bruce Burch my editor who worked doggedly to have the English Language served in this work. Having a rather casual style myself, and a rather emotional commitment to the subject matter, along with a sense of humor—Mr. Burch definitely had his hands full. Ellwood Annaheim has been working closely with my Publisher to meet the guidelines required to format this book—an intensely tedious job, to which he has brought skill and knowledge. My good friend John Balkema offered to do a complete reading as an interested bystander. John being very smart and a librarian certainly helped. I really think that he wanted to take a voice lesson after he had finished. Michael Cordovana, my mentor and dear friend for 40 years, who read rewrite after rewrite and kept telling me that there was nothing like this out there to read for voice students and professional singers in trouble with their singing. His encouragement meant everything. And lastly Marcella Calabi—a student of mine for years with a beautiful soprano voice and the mind and musicality to go along with it, who prodded me to keep going through her research and wonderful conversation on whatever subject was current in the manuscript. Marcella put the book in its first format—a format that made me very excited about a fast completion date.

Denes Striny

Introduction
Singers and How They Get That Way

"Where have all the head voices gone?"
Christa Ludwig (New York Master Class, January 1997)

In January 1997, I had the wonderful fortune of attending a master class taught by the great soprano Christa Ludwig. Twelve of the best voice teachers of Manhattan had each sent their best student to participate in the class and benefit directly from Christa's experience and insights on the human voice. After hearing the twelve students she asked one question, really a condemnation of vocal instruction today. She asked, "Where have all the head voices gone?"

This is the premise and impetus of this book. The HEAD VOICE isn't truly understood by today's vocal performer or his or her teacher and coach. It is fast becoming a lost art. This book is my explanation of the Head Voice and how to sing using its beautiful, effortless, and unconstricted style. It is my journey through wrong techniques and lengthy recovery to arrive at the true understanding of what it means to sing in the Head Voice. Only the great singers like Christa Ludwig, Birgit Nilsson, Kiri Te Kanawa, Jussi Bjoerling, Joan Sutherland, Leontyne Price, Luciano Pavarotti, and a handful of others sing in this voice. They are becoming a rarity among the new breed of performer who either rejects the texture of Head Voice or doesn't really understand how to achieve the velvety, full-voiced sound.

Do some singers just "have it" and others don't? My answer is a resounding **NO!** Luciano Pavarotti, Birgit Nilsson, Monserrat Caballe, Kiri Te Kanawa, Joan Sutherland, and Leontyne Price are not phenomenal singers from another planet. Neither were Jussi Bjoerling, Robert Merrill, Leonard Warren, Zinka Milanov, and Fiorenza Cossotto. In fact, the physical difference between great opera singers and the rest of us is **nil!**

My theory about this subject called singing originates with the day we are born. As infants, we come into the world crying, announcing that we are here and are all right. We are then hugged, fed, played with, cuddled, kissed, and touched by hospital staff and family. What a neat experience. Imagine the feeling of filling the delivery room with our sound and having people respond in this manner.

As we grow older, we yell and scream in play and even begin to think in terms of organized sound called speech, music, and singing. We get glimpses of this sound when we wail in the shower. As a choice of career, we may fantasize of having a voice that fills the Metropolitan Opera House. What an incredible reality it would be if our singing prompted people to stand up and cheer "*bravo*." Power, food, hugs; and so on . . . these are powerful rewards.

But there's another side. Somewhere between day one and year two the act of crying changes for most of us. It isn't a pleasurable sensation any longer. It is rather an expression of fear, pain, and hunger. We now hold back the shouting, controlling our feelings and our sound by constricting our muscles until we burst into tears. This is a process that continues through our learning how to speak. "**Constriction**" becomes a part of the process. If this constriction becomes too pronounced, we "choke" when we vocally express our love, our sadness, our anger.

Some people pass through these formative years without needing to constrict, without engaging muscular control to hold back speaking, yelling, or crying. For some, the wonderful feeling of producing sound supersedes the psychological need to constrict. These rare people become our natural singers, encouraged to sing since childhood. They sing in church and they sing in the school chorus and musicals. They sing the songs that use the voice in a way that encourages listeners to love them, feed them, and pay them. They sing music that is welcomed, music that is known for a particular reaction—Pavarotti singing "*O sole mio*" for instance.

In other words, **world-class voices are the ones that, by great good fortune and usually by an abundance of hard work, haven't lost what we all started with, an unconstricted voice**.

This point is very important and worth understanding. It means we no longer need to think of the great singers we admire as some sort of "*other species*" with which we can never aspire to belong. Their natural singing is an ability that we have the potential to understand and replicate. We can learn what they do naturally. Preserving our own vocal timbre and inspirational style, we can sing as they sing.

The first factor that makes a singer is **desire**. Wanting to sing is reinforced by people who tell us that we sound wonderful. Why does one young singer sound better than another does? **We are going to be better singers if our voices are definitely used in a way that involves less constriction, i. e., *more head voice***. This is the central thesis of this book and we will read much more about this. For now, the question is how can a young singer create more head voice and, therefore, less constriction?

Influences that contribute to the sheer happenstance of how a young person's body chooses to produce sound include:

- *The kind of speech one hears growing up;*
- *The kind of singing one hears growing up;*
- *The way one learns—by example or by chance—to deal with emotion and tension in the body; and*
- *The way one perceives and presents him or herself to the world.*

Listening to examples of good singing and being temperamentally suited to using one's body in a relatively unconstricted way is, in large measure, sheer luck. So are other factors, such as "being in the right place at the right time," "lucking into" good learning opportunities, and wonderful apprenticeship programs. What we are looking for, though, are **factors we can control** in an effort to become great singers.

Professional opportunities sometimes can also destroy the voice and one's hopes of singing like the greats. Lucky enough to sing in a relatively unconstricted way, a singer might find him or herself wanting—and at times, being asked—to produce more sound, to stretch his or her limits, or to try new things. Teachers, coaches, and conductors want volume or emotion or this or that. A singer willingly learns new repertoire, different styles, and new techniques, but more than likely will lose the vocal attributes that were stumbled upon in one's youth, the qualities he or she did not understand, recognize, or know enough to protect when a child. Only a few singers survive the first few years of advanced "training" and professional singing; even fewer maintain a long and healthy career.

The difference for survivors in this hectic approach to a career is this: They sing in an unconstricted way. And **the unconstricted way of singing means an active use of the head voice**. Most singers do not sing in the head voice today. But they all have the head voice available to them. *ANYONE* ***CAN*** *SING IN THE HEAD VOICE.*

Part 1: Choices

"OPERA'S LOST GENERATION OF STARS . . . a whole generation of singers seems to be missing in action. Where are the stars now in their 50's? There are precious few of them. The blight extends to some in their 40's. So what has happened? A significant cause is a lack of proper education, not only about how to sing, but about which roles are appropriate for which voices and, equally important, how to say no."

Anne Midgette, The New York Times, May 28, 2006

Chapter 1
Head Voice and Chest Voice: *Registers and Choices*

Discovery

(CD Track 1, 2, 3, 4)

In my early years as a student, the words "**head voice**" and "**chest voice**" were never mentioned. The approach that was fostered in my college years was one of hit and miss. My teacher thought it was a metaphysical approach whereby a singer, bombarded with enough information read from stacks of books on the piano, would make the right choices in producing sound. Because of this approach, I went from a *tenorino* to a bass-baritone in two years. Hindsight obviously has shown me that I made the wrong choice.

The area of the voice that my teacher concentrated on was the lower part, and one day in the studio he got my voice to drop into the chest register—an area of the voice I had never used. He was thrilled. He was a tenor who had no chest register, because it was stretched up to the top of his voice, a trait quite common with tenors. So, when he heard my booming chest voice, he was impressed and wanted me to take it one step further taking that sound all the way to the top. This was the beginning of a 20 year process to find my real voice. At age 25 after seven years of this haphazard approach, I sounded like I was 50 years old.

The rest of this story will be told later, but the short of it is that I took six-month hiatus from singing. I discovered that when I sang with principles of beauty and freedom, a beautiful tenor voice, not a bass, began to emerge. The voice that did emerge was first rate, and it had no connection to that bass-baritone voice. My friends thought I had lost my mind—why would I give up a proven commodity for something unknown? I truly don't know why, except that that other voice just did not musically satisfy me. It didn't sound or feel truthful because of the laryngeal manipulation I was using to produce the sound. When I rid myself of these muscular calisthenics, I found my voice. I found my tenor voice by myself . . . only to have the next teacher in New York muscularize it.

Experienced

Fortunately, I knew what I had done to get this far and was at least now singing in my correct voice category. My teacher in New York would tell me that he noticed that I had a problem identifying the registers; that I was always getting them confused. This assessment came from a man who had never sung nor learned to sing. But he was a PROFESSIONAL voice teacher, and so, of course, I believed him and changed my technique once again. The rescue process four years later amounted to the same process that I had gone through 10 years earlier.

Inexperienced

An interesting event happened recently. I went to a concert at a renowned summer festival. This was the last concert of the festival where the singers showed how much they had learned. Of the twenty-two singers, only two could really sing. The others sang with throaty, belted, strung-out chest voices. After the concert I spoke to one of the two good performers. She had her Ph.D. in psychology, did not read music, and had never had a voice lesson. She learned how to sing all the works she performed that night from Joan Sutherland and Kiri Te Kanawa recordings. Her singing was absolutely lovely. She had beautiful tone and her singing sounded effortless. The other twenty singers were products of every major School of Music and Conservatory in the country. How interesting and yet sadly how ironic!

Why is this voice thing so confusing? In New York, right now, I don't know of one voice teacher who understands the head voice or has a pedagogy that promotes it. Singers are being left with throaty, ugly, chest-dominant voices with limited range, and they are paying $150 an hour for this misdirection. Where is the accountability and where is the standard of sound that fosters good, healthy singing?

Here lies the problem: **there is no standard of sound**. Whatever sound a student produces by pushing, pulling, bracing, supporting, and so on is often considered his or her sound. Many people think that this is what God gave them. This is the sound that a teacher ascribes to that particular voice. There is no doubt that this sound is not like any of the great singers' sounds, or that it could become like a great singer's voice. No, the teacher thinks this particular student just wasn't "blessed" with a beautiful voice.

If a teacher actually gets a student coming into the studio with a beautiful voice, two results can occur. If the voice is beautiful enough and the teacher merely makes positive comments and plays the piano for the student, the student probably will keep that beautiful sound and become a professional singer. The youth then goes on the road as a performer singing too much to be able to continue with voice lessons. As an alternative, the voice teacher has the student work intensively to "build" the voice. A tenor then becomes a *heldentenor*; a lyric soprano becomes a dramatic soprano, and so forth. Over a period of several years this once lucky singer loses his or her beautiful free voice.

Often the reality is that a little bit of both occurs, and over a period of five years these young singers' voices diminish and we no longer hear of them. I know I paint a very grim picture, but this has happened all too often and is happening now. Each generation of singer expresses the same concern, but it seems that now we truly are at the bottom trying like Sisyphus to roll a giant rock back up the hill. Something needs to change.

Registers: What Are They?

Many people associate the head voice with a reedy thin sound with little amplitude or quality. They think that *in order to sing high one must call upon the chest voice to provide support* to the voice and to brace it. But what I have just described is a chest voice that has been stretched out to cover a person's entire vocal range. **Many teachers get these two registers—head and chest—confused**, and that is why many thought that Birgit Nilsson sang in her chest voice.

This is absolutely incorrect; she sings in the head voice. The head voice is a rich, vibrant, dynamic sound that fills out on the bottom to a velvety, dark sound and opens up at the top to a spinning, shimmering sound at any dynamic. Some performers argue saying, "But if I sing in my head voice, I won't be heard." Don't say this to famed soprano and teacher Birgit Nilsson! In my voice sessions with her, she always spoke of singing with a "slim voice, not like Eva Marton or Ghena Dimitrova who sing with a big voice." What Nilsson meant is that she sensed all the space in her throat that she was not using. She could have allowed the sound to drop back into her throat by using her chest voice, but she refused. She knew that singing like that was, to use a metaphor, using up "principal" very quickly, whereas singing in the head voice used only the "interest." She never over-manipulated or deliberately made physical space for the sound; her sound made acoustical space for itself.

Head Voice over Chest Voice

One needs to have a way of singing that transcends the conscious, mechanical level of understanding, a way that becomes almost mindless. This kind of singing relies on the reflexive action of the body to produce the note and sound. In other words, **singing must just seem to happen**.

A very good friend, international tenor John Aler, once was staying at my house in the Berkshires during performances of *Carmina Burana* at Tanglewood. One day at eight in the morning, he came into the living room and asked me to hear a high D he was preparing to sing for a selection in an upcoming concert. He sang the preceding phrase and popped into the high D with little effort producing a fantastic tone. I was so jealous that he was able to sing anything that well that early in the morning; I couldn't respond. John was able to make the sound just "seem to happen."

Teachers today continue to confuse the texture and action of the chest and *falsetto* register and continue to confuse the chest voice with the head voice. Their ears do not discern the differences, and they are not able to explain the techniques needed to sing in the head voice. The predominant miscalculation happens when a teacher or singer tries to get more *falsetto* into the chest voice. This extension attempts to increase the *falsetto* presence; however, it still leaves the voice chest-dominant and constricted. It leaves the singer no closer toward understanding how Franco Corelli had made a seamless diminuendo into his *falsetto* on a high A in "*E lucevan le stelle*," or how Monserrat Caballe can sing with such a luscious pianissimo.

So what exactly is the head voice?

The most important element to remember about the head voice and chest voice is that the **head voice does not move the larynx** to create language and sound. It allows the larynx to stay open and relaxed while changing pitch and vowel and while enunciating consonants. Conversely, **a larynx that moves is one that is constricted**; the movement constitutes a closure of the throat.

The chest voice moves the larynx with every change of pitch, vowel and consonant, making a singer's job as a chest-dominant singer a mind-boggling feat. This action involves overt muscular control that results in pushing, pulling, and bracing to hold the larynx down, to keep a modicum of energy flowing through it, and to keep it open, not totally choked-off. The sound that is produced through this effort is hardly worth the battle: shouted and blatant with no ability to sing softly. It is impossible to sing softly in that effortful texture, so the singer shifts gears into a softer texture. This shift creates a second voice, though, with neither one having anything to do with the other.

Attending a performance at the Met once, I heard a Verdi-style mezzo of the 90's singing Amneris. For my money it may as well have been Ethel Merman singing, "There's No Business like Show Business." This particular singer lauds her chest voice as the only way to sing; the more chest voice used the better. But there was not one beautiful note all night long emanating from the stage, just blood and guts. It's sad that this sound is fast becoming the standard. The rich, plumy, round mezzo sounds of days past represent just that, a thing of the past. The inappropriate chest sound of the present occurs because **no one understands the head voice or its use**. Reduced laryngeal movement is the key element that makes the head voice preferable to the chest voice for singing opera. But—try to hold the larynx still—and you will have many problems!

An important question needs to be considered. Why is the head voice better for singing opera? The answer to this all-important question is quite simple. Opera is written for a pitch range that is easily encompassed by the head voice, not the chest voice. The musical and emotional texture of the head voice makes the actual sound a musical and artistic product worth pursuing. This was understood by early composers like Verdi, Donizetti, Bellini, and Strauss—that is why they wrote for this pitch range and voice texture.

Take note of these acoustical facts. The texture of the head voice creates frequencies of 2500-3000 cycles per seconds, giving it that brilliant yet rich sound. The mean frequency of a symphony orchestra by contrast is only 700-900 cps. The chest voice creates frequencies of 900-1100 cps, not much higher than an orchestra. The human ear canal is tuned to a frequency much closer to the head voice. It is tuned to 2800 cps, making it the perfect sympathetic resonator for the head voice. We, therefore, not only hear the head voice but also feel it physically. This is no accident in the chain of human experience.

In addition to proper laryngeal placement to create this phenomenon concerning frequency, one must also sing in the language of the head voice. This means using vowels that are head voice-oriented which requires vowel placement more forward than we think possible. These vowels usually are not the same as the ones most of us use in speech. Head voice vowels must also contain all the texture of the *falsetto* as is most clearly heard in the vowel [u] and [o].

During the Victorian *Golden Age of Singing*, elocution was a standard course taught in a proper girl's finishing school or in college. Although we today make fun of Julia Child's signature expression "*bon appetite*" or Eleanor Roosevelt's speaking voice, their voices are the product of those elocution lessons; they were using the head voice for what was considered appropriate speaking. When we replicate that quality and apply it to our singing, we will have that full-voiced, velvety sound of the head voice.

The pitch range of the *falsetto*/head texture is from first line treble E-flat to the top of one's voice. Below this E-flat exists the chest register, but never above it. For every child of any age or nationality—before constriction enters—this is the way the voice works. We hear this when a child starting on the third space treble C sings downward to middle C. As a child passes from E to D, the voice drops from the head into the chest register. This is true for both male and female voices. This natural order of registration does not change with puberty; the register expands and fills out both physically and texturally. Those who maintain the freedom and order of their childhood voices, avoiding constriction, will have beautiful, full-throated operatic voices. The texture of the head and chest registers is different, and this is based on how much or how little the larynx moves/constricts. If a free, open-throated voice is singing below first line treble E-flat, its texture will be different from above that point.

Here's another observation about texture. In the last century, if people heard an operatic performer singing a popular song or a show tune, they'd laugh and make fun of the singer. The sound produced was phony and contrived. And so few operatic singers have tackled Rodgers and Hammerstein and then with limited success. Eileen Farrell was the first "crossover" vocalist; she could sing pops and jazz, as well as opera. Her operatic voice, though, did not last long after this, but her pops voice was still wonderful. She adjusted her technique and texture to accommodate the many styles she performed. For opera, though, the head voice is truly the most successful and desirable sound.

Today almost every major opera singer is singing "crossover." What has changed? Is it the public's ear or the singer's voice? Today we would laugh if we heard Renata Tebaldi, Renata Scotto, or Maria Callas sing "I Could Have Danced All Night" as a serious performance piece with their classically trained voices. It would be hilarious and even ridiculous. Today the singer's voice is not flexible but is changing from an operatic style and sound to a non-operatic one. This sound is well able to convey the word in a way that is acceptable to more people, but this change involves allowing the chest voice more dominance in the singing, thereby bringing it closer to speech. This technique doesn't work well in opera and so "crossover" performers need to crossover to that musical form and stay there. It will help raise the standard in both art forms.

This does not mean that the operatic singer must use a belting voice, even though at times it may seem so. Do you remember our Verdi-style mezzo of the 90's? This shift to a "**mixed voice**" is well and good, but only if it **stays out of the realm of opera**. Unfortunately, the public's aesthetic taste has been blurred, and our perception of operatic sound is in a state of limbo. **The language of the head voice is disappearing**. The vowel sounds are being produced back in the throat where everyday speech occurs, so the sounds are becoming broad and blatant. Throaty, gargled singing is replacing the standard of round, focused, spinning, and beautiful singing.

Head Voice

The best way to begin understanding the head voice is to listen to exemplars: Sutherland, Nilsson, Moffo, Price, Merrill, Pinza, Ghiaurov, Netrebko,

Cappucilli, Warren, Chernov, Cossotto, Ludwig, Bartoli, Bjoerling, Gigli, Matilla, Swenson, Corelli, Te Kanawa, and Pavarotti. These great singers past and present sing or sang in the head voice. Because of the way they sing, their sounds are individual and honest and uphold the **highest operatic standard—the standard of the head voice.**

The most important and fundamental point to remember is that we already possess a head voice in the same way that we already have a chest voice. All our energy, though, does not flow into the head voice, as it should when we sing. It is dissipated going into a mixture with the chest voice. But when we sing in the head voice, we sing in a particular and appropriate way. When we sing in the chest voice, we sing in a very different way. We are capable of hearing and understanding the difference and of reproducing the head voice.

A few years ago when I was singing with the Santa Fe Opera, I became acquainted with one of America's current lyric sopranos who before this time had been a lyric coloratura with great career potential. She told me one day that she did not have a notion of what the head voice was. I could hardly believe her, but in further conversation I realized she truly did not have a clue. She also explained she had been having problems with her notes above high B-natural and that she was thinking of switching to lyric soprano repertoire.

I told her that I did not think that her choice was the right solution and that she should try to discover what she was doing wrong. Instead, she should discover how to sing in the head voice and produce the high notes with ease and beauty. I further mentioned that if she did not take the time to worry about notes over B-natural, that she might continue to lose notes and eventually become a tenor. This problem was never corrected and, even though still in her prime, this opera performer currently sings very little. When she does perform, she is extremely nervous. Every high note is such an anxiety-producing event that she no longer enjoys the music. Many times her audience can't either.

Chest Voice: Muscle Power

One of the predominant pedagogies taught in the world today can be summarized in the words of author and teacher Douglas Stanley:

> It is futile to tell the student to open his throat, since such localized control is physiologically impossible. Such directions, however, as "go for the throat," "form the vowels farther back," "hold the throat firm," "work with the throat," "balance the work done in the production of the tone with firmness of the throat," "start the tone with the throat," "don't let the throat collapse as you ascend the scale," "tense the throat the moment of attacking the tone," etc. will with constant repetition convey a definite meaning.

A definite meaning these instructions will convey and also a definite sound. It will produce a throaty sound! Since the turn of the 20th century when the laryngoscope was invented by Manuel Garcia he began his study of the voice and vocal production. Many voice teachers have felt that because sound is produced in the throat, the sensation should be there also, and therefore, the energy should be directed there. Vocal production from this location, though, negates beautiful singing, and sound produced in this manner is not beautiful. It can be musical but it is not inherently beautiful.

Many voice students who sing improperly in this way listen to great singers and think that God has given those performers a voice that He didn't give to them. Very rarely do they think more positively: "I don't sing the way X sings, but if I did, I would sound very much the same." We don't equate the basic sound of our voice with the commodity that is changeable. **Yes, our voices can be improved, but as long as the manner of singing is chest-dominant, this type of change will never occur.**

Most causes of vocal tension in singers are directly related to the individual's level of technical skill. Inefficient vocal technique creates tensions not only in the vocal instrument but also in the external muscles that must then overcompensate. Therefore, the very goal that a singer pursues in vocal training—a chest-dominant sound with a great deal of laryngeal movement and counter muscular movement to compensate—can itself be stressful.

What to Trust

What or who then should we trust if current vocal training is suspect? The writer/philosopher Ralph Waldo Emerson said it most succinctly:

"Trust Thyself."

Singing is a natural phenomenon. There are common sense occurrences that we can tap into to discover more natural singing. Remember the performer who learned to sing by listening to Sutherland and Te Kanawa recordings? If we emulate what she did, we would be on the right path toward singing as she sings.

Tension begets tension, but good singing will relax that tension. When there is tension in the voice, it is transmitted into sound, an unpleasant sound. We must trust ourselves so that our minds and bodies can work it out. The body will usually show the mind how it is able to work by using reflexes, but the mind must permit it to happen first. We must permit the body the freedom to work naturally. If we plant a flower seed, we will get a flower.

The more we watch and listen to our bodies with a kind of detached interest, allowing our body to lead the way, the more we will learn. We need to let this process direct our voice, rather than engage in over-manipulation and contrived control of the vocal instrument and the accompanying muscles. The correct process, I'll repeat, involves the head voice, and it is best to stay out of its way.

RELAX!!
RELAX!!!
AAAHHHH

Chapter 2
Breathing—No Big Deal

Choices

We know that singing is a mysterious and wonderful process whereby any pitch, intensity, and vowel that we imagine in our mind's ear can become an actual sound. Our minds translate that imagined goal into innumerable physical adjustments in the throat and elsewhere, controlling many aspects of the vibrating "valve" in order to make that sound happen.

It is critically important to realize that the sound texture discussed earlier, in fact, is the primary controller of the vocal valve. We have basically two choices: the **head voice texture** or the **chest voice texture**. To make a conscious choice between these two textures, we need to have experienced the sensations associated with each one first. That, in essence, is the learning process. When the association is learned, hearing that texture in our minds and calling upon our bodies to produce it is all we have to do, consciously, to select our choice. It boils down to recognizing the sensation of the sound texture and trusting that recognition to do the work. The texture controls the valve, either allowing breath through or inhibiting it!

Choosing between a head voice texture and a chest voice texture affects every other aspect of our singing in fundamental ways. From that point this chapter examines the much-discussed phenomenon of breathing.

Study voice with more than one teacher or at a school with several voice faculty members and you may hear any of the following:

- Exhalation is an active process and inhalation is a relaxation.

- In correct breathing, *the rib cage:*

a) is expanded and remains that way;
b) is left alone;
c) expands and contracts.

- In correct breathing, *the abdomen:*

  a) moves out on the inhale and in on the exhale;
  b) moves in on the inhale and out on the exhale;
  c) moves out on the inhale and then should resist collapse.

- In correct breathing, *the lower back:*

  a) expands and contracts;
  b) doesn't expand and contract;
  c) feels like it expands and contracts but really doesn't.

- Musical intention is enough; the body will execute.

- If you breathe correctly, correct singing will follow, but not the other way around.

- There is no correct breathing technique.

- If you sing correctly, correct breathing will follow, but not the other way around.

- Inhalation is an active process and exhalation is a relaxation.

- Correct breathing is of primary importance for good singing technique.

- How you breathe doesn't matter.

- To carry out musical intention we need muscular control in the breathing process.

What is going on here? Why is there confusion and obvious contradiction? Why is there all this attention to breathing in the first place?

Breath is certainly necessary for singing, and the desire to understand and control the process of singing leads easily to a fascination with breathing. The breathing mechanism is tangible and can easily be learned and developed properly for singing. It involves large muscles that are relatively easy to control; they can be easily seen, felt, and manipulated. A teacher can poke a voice student in the abdomen, hold it, squeeze it, sit on it, stand on it, and I'm sure much more.

One of the oddest exercises I've heard involves pushing the piano around the room with the diaphragm. Lovely!

It is so tempting for singers to think and hope that by getting the breathing "right" by overtly controlling this large musculature, they can find the magic formula for a beautiful voice. In interviews and books, many of the great performers have talked and written about breathing. But, unfortunately, the discussions of breathing differ from one singer to another. If good singers disagree with each other on the value and techniques of breathing, finding the right answer is almost impossible.

Effect: Not the Same as Cause

The solution is to recognize what else great singers have to say about breath control and what they do to achieve it. They talk about the feeling of resonance in the face and head; they talk about the sound as happening somewhere "out there." They also tend to talk about what happens simultaneously when one sings. These points are very significant but the voice student wants to know what to do, not what to feel. For the student, how does breathing relate to the singing process?

Great singing involves freedom from constriction, freedom from added tension. Freedom from constriction means little or no overt, consciously- controlled muscularity. This muscularity can be felt and is easily identified, and for the voice student it comes with a satisfying thought that he or she is doing something. Ironically, though, to "feel something" isn't correct singing. Freedom from constriction is a wonderful state in which a singer is aware of *the absence of excessive tension*, the absence of feeling. Freedom in the mouth and throat is a sensation in which the mouth drops open, the jaw is tensionless, the soft palate hangs tensionless, and one may even start to drool. The same position of the palate and the jaw also can happen when one is asleep in front of the TV. The great tenor Enrico Caruso said, "In order to sing well, you must sing with the mouth of an idiot." So, feeling muscularity is quite wrong in good singing.

Great singers then do not have many easily identifiable sensations to refer to when discussing singing and breathe control. They don't feel the larynx while they sing; they don't feel anything in their throats; they don't feel much in their mouths. Much of what they do feel is "out there" which is a hard to define entity. Great singing definitely isn't a sensation derived from tense muscles, but the diaphragm and the intercostal muscles, nonetheless, are critical in any explanation. These muscles are large, visible, and palpable, and their action can always be felt, seen, and identified, even though they are not painfully tense. So, great singers can talk about their breathing as well as the feeling "out there!"

Does that mean that breathing is the element that makes everything else about singing happen, the horse that draws the cart? Absolutely not! Texture controls the valve! All of the ways of breathing mentioned thus far are physically possible. Moreover, many of them have at some time worked for some great singers. In fact, experimentation has shown that the total volume of air moved in and out of the lungs is essentially the same whether a singer uses "thoracic" or "diaphragmatic" breathing. The differences are not considered significant by pulmonary specialists, even those familiar with the phenomenon of singing.

The respiratory valve is the primary controller of the breath. If there is constriction in the pathway of the breath, breathing will be labored. This valve concerns the opening and closure of the vocal cords in the larynx inside the throat. How the great performers sing (and the sound/texture which is the product of that singing) and how we sing (and the resulting sound/texture) is the real issue.

Constricted Singing—Manipulated Breathing

Think about the way we breathe before lifting a heavy object; think about pushing that piano around with the abdomen. It calls for the rib cage area and/or the belly to stiffen, to brace and, therefore, to resist the constriction about to take place. Most of the day fortunately we don't apply that kind of action when we breathe. The operation is smoother, less extreme, and quite involuntary. The diaphragm, a muscle positioned below the lungs and above the stomach, moves downward upon inhalation with the abdomen being pushed out of the way. This downward movement then increases the space in the lungs, creating a vacuum and forcing air inward in order to equalize the pressure. In exhalation the smooth effort involved in those movements relaxes, the diaphragm rises with the chest then returning to a resting state. If we need to use the "last bits" of air in the lungs, the reserve or auxiliary breath, the diaphragm obliges us by rising further than normal to push air out with the lung space generally becoming smaller. Afterwards, everything returns to the resting state. Breathing involves this constant, involuntary, fluid movement; there is no rigid tension but a constant smooth change in the length of this important muscle.

But if one thinks that singing involves bracing the breath, tensing the abdomen, expanding the rib cage, resulting in lifted shoulders and chest expansion, resisting collapse for all it's worth, then he or she is choosing a rigid kind of muscular activity that conforms to muscular tone. Remove the description of the shoulders and the expanded chest and one is describing the muscular activity that conforms to singing with the chest voice. The whole body braces as if ready to lift a heavy piece of furniture. True, a breath has been taken and singing can now take place. But if we sing in this manner, the body is in a constant state of rigidity on the verge of suffocating because we are holding the breath. It's impossible to sing in a state of living *rigor mortis*.

There are, of course, degrees of difference here. For example, one can sing with an expanded rib cage and a tucked-in abdomen, and still sing well; there are many very good, even famous singers who use this breathing approach. Even at its best, this kind of singing usually has a certain element of tightness in the vocal texture and in the high notes so that the sound does not blossom. Far worse is singing with tension in the larynx. Here one may be doing irreparable damage to the vocal mechanism itself. When we sing in the head voice, though, we are encouraging the body to function in a certain way, a relaxed way, and tension anywhere in the breath is quite incompatible with a quality head voice sound.

A useful analogy here is a balloon that we inflate and then gradually release air to make squeaky noises. To produce the sound we must use the neck of the balloon as a valve, pulling it to the sides to narrow the aperture. With the contorted neck, we can begin making the odd and irreverent sounds. When we adjust this valve one way, we tend to lose all the air; when we adjust it too tightly, we stop the flow of air altogether. If the valve is tightly closed and we still want to produce sound, we must press on the balloon, thus increasing air pressure which overcomes the closure of the valve. The greater the tension on the valve, the greater the need for pressure to overcompensate. Notice that this pressure is tension against the resisting valve. While the original "intent" of the balloon wall is to shrink, now it has to be braced against resistance.

In the vocal mechanism, we have a far more complicated system, but the balloon analogy still holds true. Here the vocal folds can lengthen and thicken at the same time. Neither one of these processes necessarily causes constriction; neither process requires excessive pressure or force from the breathing mechanism. But if pitch and texture are controlled by overt muscularity anywhere in the throat, the valve is said to be constricted; in fact, it is bracing. We don't want this excessive pressure. The valve is mimicking the same process that the large musculature in the torso uses to assist in lifting a heavy object. It becomes necessary to add breath pressure to continue the sound. If the valve is constricted in the same way, overt muscular activity will be triggered to occur.

Laryngeal constriction or excess holding in the vocal folds causes the same result: greater tension and pressure occurring until the valve is too tight to operate. The singer chokes; the tone stops, or breaks off to the *falsetto*. We've all heard how some performers try to make an impressive ending to an aria by "blasting the walls down" like the trumpets of Jericho with a final high note only to choke. It's not a pretty sound. We as the audience respond almost as strongly as the singer does to this kind of disaster.

So the primary issue in vocal production isn't the breath alone, but rather the vocal valve being placed in an unconstricted environment of the total breathing mechanism through the choice of an unconstricted texture of sound. We've seen that a constricted valve *requires* excess breath pressure. If a singer feels that he or she is working too hard when breathing, reducing the breath pressure will not help until valve constriction passes. Trying to retrain one's abdominal muscles will not address the problem; that is not getting to the heart of the problem. Breathing is blowing air through an unconstricted valve, and singing should feel the same way.

Many voice teachers give lip service to the idea of an unconstricted throat. However, when their aesthetics of sound favors the kind of texture that is produced by a constricted valve, the unconstricted throat is impossible. Despite a dedication to the concept of an unconstricted valve, they are in practice still teaching the use of a constricted valve mechanism. Unfortunately, throat constriction **always** leads to stress in the rest of the body as well as in the singer's emotional state. The irony is that this stress encourages more constriction. Many singers find this vicious cycle impossible to break. The basic method of producing tone is faulty and not free.

Unconstricted Singing; Unconstricted Breathing—HEAD VOICE

Every function of the body that controls our lives should operate without unnecessary tension. If tension infiltrates one function, the whole body is debilitated. Thank goodness most body functions operate below our conscious control and are produced involuntarily; they save us from the temptation to manipulate and overtly control them. I once had a student who firmly believed that if she did not consciously "will" her breathing, it would not happen. Imagine the constriction in her body and her singing.

Anything that inhibits the natural flow of breathing is constricting. Natural is the way we breathe all day every day, unlike when lifting that piano. Constricting and bracing which occurs in bad singing produces a far less beautiful tone. High notes are more difficult to sing, and general tightness in the body occurs. We have evolved over time to breathe in a moving and fluid way. When the voice is free of rigidity, the breath work occurs about a foot and a half away from the singing process. The singer produces that "out there" sensation of head voice texture. The breath work supplies the air and the energy without interfering with the singing process. When the method of tone production in the larynx is free of holding, there is no need to brace the breathing apparatus against the valve and force the breath through the vocal folds by applying extra pressure.

Such a mutually free relationship between the singing process and the breathing process sounds positively idyllic, but it is so rare these days. **The only way to establish such a mutually free relationship is to sing in the HEAD VOICE.** Those who sing in this manner with its lack of muscular sensation do not realize that IT IS THEIR TEXTURE OF SOUND THAT IS REGULATING THE BREATH. It is worth repeating what has been mentioned elsewhere in this book: **chest voice singing is constricted singing with the incorrect texture!** The chest voice musculature tips and raises the larynx, pushing inward on the vocal folds, causing constriction in the vocal "valve." Singing in the chest voice creates that situation where pressurized breathing becomes necessary to overcome the resistance in the valve.

The head voice musculature, on the other hand, does not cause constricted movement in the larynx. Moreover, that musculature sensation is below the level of conscious control. By definition, you cannot give your body orders that cause tightness like a bodybuilder flexing every muscle possible in the final moment of his or her presentation and still choose the head voice for singing.

Singing in the head voice with unconstricted breathing is the element that needs attention. It is natural breathing, normal. It can be subverted by unconsciously poor body use or by bad training, **but in everyday breathing the body tends to find effortless movement.** Singing in the head voice can be—and usually is—subverted by the cultural norms of the singing we hear and learn and for all the physiological reasons to "push" already mentioned.

If our natural tendencies and the desired processes have been subverted, we need to know how to retrain ourselves. What new or corrective orders can we give our bodies to rectify bad habits? We all long to know what to do to make our singing better. If breath does not come first, and if the head voice musculature is below the level of conscious control, what really does come first? What can we choose; what can we control; what can we do?

WE CAN CHOOSE THE PROPER SOUND TEXTURE. Once we identify it by experience in the studio with our ear of imagination, we can learn to hear the sound texture that comes only with the head voice and train our bodies to produce that sound. This advice, this sound, this technique will adjust the valve, and ask the body to supply the energy by supplying the right amount of breath. As we experience more and more reliably the sensations of freedom that go with this wonderfully efficient use of breath, we can use our muscle memory of those sensations as triggers, too. We can simply *feel* our voice as unconstricted energy. Selecting tone and texture are important, but they will seem to become secondary.

If this sounds too simplistic to believe, it is not. Very few singers perform in this manner, and we easily recognize the names of the ones who do: Bjoerling, Caballe, Nilsson, Sutherland, and others. The energy in their singing is directed, and the processes are coordinated by a fantastic computer, the brain. It knows what to do, how much energy to supply, how long and how thick the vocal chords must be, how the throat should feel during the process; and it knows what not to do to give the sound its full potential. We must stay out of the **computer's** way and let it perform the functions and adjustments needed to sing properly. We can't over-think singing at performance time; we must practice to enhance muscular memory and generate the habit of singing correctly, the head voice habit.

If we have problems singing, we may not consciously remember what it felt like to be free of excess physical tension. As we relearn to sing in the head voice, some attention to releasing the constrictions elsewhere in the body may enhance and speed up our learning. But be careful not to put the cart before the horse. With the valve acting as the primary controller of the breath, singing in the head voice will give us ninety percent of the improvement we want.

In this context, it is useful to recognize that the greatest singers have not been the specimens of perfect athletic shape or health. What does this observation tell us? It reminds us that flexible bodies and aerobic condition are not the explanations for these singers' efficient use of breath. Could it be that these singers are so used to deep breathing that their bodies use the oxygen in each breath more efficiently? NO! Scientists report that if we are not in good shape, and particularly if we are overweight, we use oxygen less efficiently. Then, do singers have larger lungs than the rest of us? Larger than who? Larger than another singer the same size who heaves and pants and bellows? Again, NO! That is not the explanation for their success. The answer is that they sing in the head voice.

If I'm Aiming for Freedom from Constriction, Why Am I Running Out of Breath?

The sound of great singers only requires a certain amount of breath, no more. Their vocal valves do not require braced, pressurized breathing. In other words, neither large volumes of oxygen nor high pressure is necessary for good, efficient singing. Great singers breathe out smoothly and without effort as they sing. The relatively small amount of air they exhale, under relatively little pressure, is all translated into sound and so **in great singing, breath becomes synonymous with sound**. There is no waste; there is no costly tension. **No waste and no tension: these are basic attributes of HEAD VOICE sound production.**

If we have studied voice at all, we already know that we can run out of breath for one of two reasons: wasting it, or not taking enough air in the first place.

When we discover our head voice and make a change from the chest-dominant to a head-dominant sound production, we sing with less and less constriction in the throat, i.e., the valve is less tight. But we still can have the bad habit of pressurizing the exhalation, forcing air against expected resistance in the vocal chords. In fact, as long as there is still a strong component of chest voice in the sound production, a signal is sent to the breathing mechanism to pressurize. The result of this excess pressure is muscle tension and air leakage. When a balance is regained in breathing and the head voice suddenly controls sound production, the air leak will stop.

All the various ways we use our breath-related muscles to push, hold, or brace have one point in common: **a quality of muscle tension** that is **difficult to release quickly**. In the breath process the most important step is the "release." If the exhalation is overly muscular, it is hard to release that tension thus allowing the air to be sucked into the lungs more efficiently. With a natural release, the diaphragm lowers which creates air pressure in the lung lower than the world outside. Air is drawn in involuntarily rather than our consciously sucking the air in. The difference involves tension-free exertion and a faster reaction time. The environment creates the inhalation, not the muscles. Conversely, if the inhalation involves **holding to resist collapse**, the exhalation will be awkward and tense, also.

Tight or braced muscular singing is tiring, and only a moment of release provides a critical element of rest in the middle of such an activity. (Ironically this way of singing is the most tiring and also the one method of breathing in which it is the most difficult to rest.) Without that rest, the body tends to become tighter and tighter. This incorrect muscular activity is another way that the cycle of tension-begetting-tension is perpetuated. If we sing with a chest-dominant vocal technique, we must practice longer and more intensely to achieve even relatively quick catch-breaths. We must train our breathing muscles to "pop back out" from their held-in exhalation position. These catch breaths are not a true release but rather a different muscular activity, merely in an opposite direction. The overall muscular rest is not truly achieved.

There is an important difference between the concept of "release" and "relax." The body is active all the time, but with truly "relaxed" muscles, we would fall over on the stage; that's not what we want. With "released," fluid movement, the breathing apparatus has a much easier job. If we get carried away in our singing and push a bit, it is still easier to release and return to a resting state. With correct technique the muscles are actually resting a great deal of the time! When we inhale, exhaling back to the resting state is not an effort; it's a little vacation. When we exhale past the resting state, expelling some of the reserve air, inhaling to return to the resting state is still "a little vacation." This process can't be achieved with a chest-dominant voice. "Resting" muscles and efficient breathing is achieved only with the head voice.

Just as we cannot really "relax" without falling over, we don't want to equate singing in the head voice with being low-energy performing. We want to sing with passion! We want a wide dynamic and emotional range. We want to apply energy to our singing. As we develop head voice, we will learn to breathe without clutching, pushing, and bracing. The head voice sound tells us what we need to do.

Chest and head voice use energy and muscles in very different ways. For a singer, used to using the chest voice, head voice production seems elusive. When Birgit Nilsson was a young student at the Stockholm Conservatory, her teacher told her he thought she sounded "like a steam boat coming down the river." For three years she brightened her voice trying to rid herself of the hooty quality, but she almost lost her voice At that point she realized that the steam boat *was* Birgit Nilsson. Obviously she didn't continue with that sound; it took her ten years to regain the head voice.

The head voice Julia Child and Eleanor Roosevelt spoke with is the same head voice that Jesse Norman, Joan Sutherland, and Birgit Nilsson have in their singing. The velvety texture of their voices is the quality of head voice production. When the symbiosis of intention, breathing muscles, and the larynx occurs, concerns about breathing simply go away. We can finally focus on the music, shaping the musical phrases by riding on the quality of the sound. One cannot sing *legato* without using the head voice. And this same flowing energy transfers "bracing breath" into "sustaining breath," which is feeding the sound. When one sings in this manner, every student says, "Oh! Breathing is No Big Deal!"

Chapter 3
All the Stuff You Want:
Pitch, Text, Musicality, Carrying Power

Pitch

Think about the analogies that we tend to use to describe different pitches. "High" and "Low," for example, are inescapably fixed in our musical vocabulary. But if we are looking at a piano, why not say "right" and "left"? If we are thinking of a stringed instrument, why not say "short" and "long" or "thin" and "thick"? If we want to be even vaguely accurate about it, why not say "fast" and "slow," referring to the vibration speed?

The spatial analogy of "high" and "low," arbitrary as it is, has been imbued with meaning for centuries. It has infiltrated our imagery of pitch, including our visualization on the written page, the hand gestures made when conducting a chorus, and the whole-body gestures made in dance, "acting out" a melody.

Now consider the set of sensations that are typically associated with producing different pitches in singing. The spatial analogy of "high" and "low" unfortunately tends to fit here, too. Sing a "high" note and the larynx will want to rise. As the larynx rises, unequally in front and back, it tilts, causing the respiratory tract to become contorted and tense. In order to make room for a rising larynx, the pharynx has to spread apart in the back of the throat. The mouth will mirror this spread condition. (We've already addressed resisting this tendency to rise.) The soft palate domes up, also. In order to dome up, though, the soft palate has to tighten.

Conversely, think about singing a very low pitch. Who has not seen a bass-baritone push his whole head down into his collar like an intimidated turtle to get "low" enough? The tension on the larynx and every related mechanism under this kind of vertical pressure is enormous. The spatial imagery of "high" happens to fit with these occurrences but does nothing to counter tension; it isn't really to blame. Singing in the chest voice is at fault here.

When singing, the pitch of sound is a function of the speed with which the edges of the vocal cords are vibrating in a column of air. The single factor most responsible for that speed is the thickness of those edges. For higher pitches the edges are thin; for lower pitches the edges are thicker. The vocal mechanism is very complicated, but this book needn't sound like a medical text. In defining registers, though, the head voice phenomenon and the chest voice phenomenon are associated with different components of the vocal musculature. The *cricoids*, the muscles that control the thickness of the edges of the vocal cords by pulling them towards the back of the larynx or letting them thicken forwards, belong to a head voice musculature. In other words, **pitch is the product of the head voice or *falsetto* mechanism.**

Does that mean that when most singers produce a pitch, they are utilizing this mechanism? Unfortunately that isn't the case. We can affect vibration of the vocal cords in a number of ways. Pushing the larynx up and tightening everything in sight does "work." We can also make the edges of the vocal cords shorter or tenser and that affects the pitch. Create the imagery of a vibrating string, again; we can raise the pitch by making the string thinner, shorter, or tauter. Considering the structure of the vocal mechanism, the efficient way to raise the pitch is to make the vocal cords thinner. But it's not the only way.

It's not the only way, one might add, if one is satisfied with imperfect pitch. Producing pitch via the chest voice is always "around the pitch" but never really "on pitch." There are a number of reasons for this. One reason is that the inefficient functioning of the vocal mechanism is a real hindrance to free vibration in the cords. Another reason is that general respiratory tract constriction closes off the resonating chambers that produce the high-frequency overtones. It is these overtones that create the "full sound" we associate with a singer being fundamentally "on pitch."

Another reason for poor pitch when singing in chest voice is that there are limits as to how high the larynx can be pushed and how tightly the mouth and throat can be spread. When the limits of tension are reached on any given pitch, that pitch begins to sag. When the limit of the laryngeal movement is reached, a performer is at the end of his or her pitch range, and it becomes increasingly difficult to go any farther.

The condition and increase of three factors—tension, chest tone which builds up in the voice, and the rising larynx—create a vicious cycle for singers, resulting in the loss of high notes, typically pitches above A-flat, that once were available. Cs, C#s, and Ds in the middle of the voice range become flat because of the amount of tension exerted by the chest voice.

When the **head voice** is introduced to singers for the first time, they are amazed that pitch is obtained in a way quite different from what they thought. Pitch no longer involves that muscular pushing of the throat with the respiratory tract closed down. Pitch now becomes a product of acoustics, like a violinist who barely touches a string to get a harmonic. There is no pressure and no pushing, even for the highest notes. One's first experience of singing high notes with the **head voice**, devoid of tension and contortion in the throat, is like a miracle. How much more so is the experience of "spinning out" pianissimo high notes floating into every corner of the opera house?

A New Way of Hearing

The experience of singing pitches in the head voice brings with it a new way of hearing. At least three aspects of hearing will change: how pitch is perceived in our mind, how we hear orchestral, piano, and other vocal pitches in the context of the music we are making, and how we perceive and understand sounds made by others, especially the great singers.

In chest-voice dominated sound production, there are strong physical sensations of movement in the larynx (tension in the throat from attempting to hold the larynx still) and constriction throughout the vocal mechanism. We may be so used to these sensations that we are not consciously aware of them; they are part of our perception of a normal state of being. These sensations are there, but when we shift to a head voice mechanism, the change is startling. As the sensations of constriction and contortion drop away, replaced by "nothing," we may suddenly feel cast adrift. The guideposts of physical sensation are no longer there and this in turn has an affect on our hearing.

After singing with chest-voice dominant production for a long time, we will have built up a set of **associations** between pitches in our mind and sensations of tightness in our body. The associations *seem* like a direct link between our mind's "ear" and our throat. Whether we have taken the time to verbalize it or not, we may think that the principal activity of producing a pitch is actuation of the fundamentals of that pitch right at the cords. This thought seems to make sense, too. If the larynx is in the throat, why can't we "feel it" there? Talk of overtones and formants seems foreign or at most secondary to the sound, and so we may think they are frosting on the cake. But these qualities of sound are important, too.

When we lose the sensation of a direct link between the throat and pitch through the discovery of head voice, we may find ourselves entirely at a loss for a while. After this discovery many voice students experience a week or two when they are not confident in producing a desired pitch. When I play a note on the piano for a student to sing in this stage of development, the correct pitch always comes forth with clarity and direction. The student just doesn't fully understand how this is happening in light of this new technique.

Singers who previously have been good at identifying pitches suddenly find themselves saying, "What was that note?" and are astonished with the answer.

They also begin gesturing vaguely toward the head and begin saying things like: "I'm hearing somewhere other than where I used to." They eventually decide they must trust this new way of hearing; they must trust their inner "ear" to imagine the sound they want to produce. Imagining this sound without the comfortably familiar but limiting crutch of the old muscular associations seems much more abstract than before.

Some students also find themselves much more aware of the overtones in a pitch they are matching when they sing with the head voice. One student talked of tuning to the overtones rather than simply matching the fundamental of a desired pitch. This stage of vocal growth is an odd sensation for a while, but it does result in a more finely honed sense of pitch with a great deal of freedom.

"Tuning in" to these aspects of sound also affects how we hear other singers. Learning a head-voice based technique has much to do with hearing a texture that is beautiful, rich and ringing with overtones, as well as with giving ourselves the freedom to produce that sound. As we become more familiar with this new sound and the method of producing it, we also begin to understand what the great singers actually do to produce that sound. We begin to identify register choices that other singers are making, and this affects how we react to what we hear. Both our awareness and appreciation of this thrilling new sound increases. **(Beware! You may become harder to please!)**

Hearing isn't enough; our direct experience of this new sound production is crucial. **Until we can produce the sound of the head voice, we will not identify it in others.** Learning to produce the sound and learning to hear the sound go together.

Getting the Words Across

"What do you read, my lord?"
"Words, words, words."
"What is the matter, my lord?"
"Between who?"
"I mean, the matter that you read, my lord."
Hamlet II, ii-190

Text is a topic that raises passion among singers, coaches, and other colleagues in the profession of vocal and choral music. It's important to analyze closely what is really involved in conveying the meaning of a piece of vocal music. First, recognize that there are at least two components to meaning in vocal music: articulate meaning (denotation and diction) and inarticulate meaning (connotation). In addition humans recognize a quality of emotion and meaning (tone and expression) in creating beauty, whether it is visual or aural beauty. Books have been written about emotion and meaning in music; centuries of discussion have been exhausted on the topic. Arguments about the programmatic elements and the nonverbal messages in purely instrumental music have been presented for generations. The component of text in vocal music doesn't eliminate the nonverbal components; it only adds complexity to the same discussion. There also is a related question concerning the purely verbal component of singing: must it be speech-like?

First let's address the element of meaning found through aural beauty. Unfortunately, much of the singing occurring today is chest-dominant and simply ugly. Because of its shrill quality and the incorrect technique leading to constriction, today's singing has an element of physical tension that communicates itself to the audience. In our hyperactive times, that rough-edged sound is frequently thought to be exciting. But this product of tension does not inspire the expansion of thought and feeling that gives aural beauty meaning.

I remember well a performance at the Met of *Ariadne auf Naxos* with Monserrat Caballe singing her first Ariadne. I had just finished a production of the same opera, singing the role of Bacchus, so I was very familiar with the words and the music. Caballe sang perhaps fifty percent of the words; the rest was simply a string of the most gorgeous vowel sounds I had ever heard. The audience, rightfully so, went wild. Caballe gave a bouquet of flowers thrown to her to the prompter for the assistance she provided.

If an ordinary performer in a coach's studio were to sing excerpts from *Ariadne auf Naxos* as Caballe had done, that singer would be called on the carpet for "not singing the words." Why? The answer lies in the fact that the ordinary singer's sound does not have the inarticulate meaning imbued in the musical sound. It wouldn't be beautiful, as Caballe had sung on the stage. Without that type of meaning, we at least would need specific verbal intelligibility to compensate, or we would have nothing! Unable to show a singer how to produce this inarticulate meaning, many coaches insist on the latter as a close approximation. Caballe does not "get away with" something that a coach would insist on from a lesser singer just because she's a "star." She is communicating *meaning* in an entirely *different way*.

Even in speech the "tone of voice" is an important part of context for humans and animals alike. It's well known that in everyday life we often do not hear or "pick up" every word, but we, nonetheless, have far fewer misunderstandings than we might because of context. Our brains are constantly leaping to conclusions about what has been said, filling in the blanks, based on context. Context includes words that are individually understood, but it also vitally includes meaning conveyed by tone.

With constriction in the vocal mechanism, the voice is terribly limited. It becomes largely impossible for a singer to express the nuances of meaning via "tone of voice" alone. For the ordinary singer, syllable-by-syllable enunciation is the only vehicle of meaning available. The extraordinary singer uses technique, diction, and expression to produce an extraordinary sound synonymous with aural beauty.

If diction is the only vehicle available for most of us, it becomes excruciatingly important. We now return to the question of speech-like singing. Elsewhere in this book it's been reported that when we sing in the head voice, we are singing with a set of vowels most people are not used to hearing. It is a different "language." These vowels are not the ones used in speech, but are a parallel set appropriate for singing in the head voice. (Remember the *Golden Age of Singing* and the elocution lessons of Child and Roosevelt.) These vowels have the high overtones and the acoustical formation that is, in a way, both the cause and effect of the head voice texture. Are the head voice vowels intelligible? Yes, but they require an adjustment by the listener who is accustomed to a chest-voice vowel set. Because the product is a gorgeous sound, this is an adjustment that the ordinary listener is willing to make.

It takes time for a singer to develop the head voice technique. The singer must learn to sustain all of the vowels without popping back into a chest dominant sound. Rather than pop back into the chest for the [i] and [e] vowels, for example, a singer who is in the process of learning the head voice technique will frequently modify the vowels with an [u] based texture. But a singer with a fully developed head voice technique is consistent in correctly producing the vowel set. The vowel sounds are clear and easily distinguishable and can only be truly understood and appreciated when performed.

The phenomenon of recorded music, and particularly of amplified music, has altered many listeners' expectations concerning the palette of sung sounds. Very few singers and teachers actually know how free the voice can be and when it is free how forward the sound is to be almost outside the body, "out there," out of the throat. This topic will be discussed in the section on vocal "carrying power," but it's worth mentioning here in the context of a discussion about speech-like singing. The only way to make purely speech-like vowels carry in a large hall, over an orchestra, is to use amplification. Another way to achieve this clarity of text is to shout, but even that doesn't work all the time. Besides, who wants to hear that type of sound?

If we sing in the chest voice, we are using the vowels that most of us use for speech. It costs us our true legato and the true beauty of the voice, of the easy high notes and the soft high notes. Singing with speech vowels in the chest voice is "classical belting." There is a place for belting; different repertoires call for an appropriate sound quality and for the technique that produces it.

Throughout this book, though, I have been on a soap box preaching head voice as the right way to sing, i.e., the right way to sing opera. This isn't necessarily the technique of jazz or musical theater, not necessarily for folk or for any type of singing that utilizes amplification. *Not necessarily*, but head voice makes all these styles more interesting, as in the work of Mariah Carey, Ella Fitzgerald, Roberta Flack, and Frank Sinatra. The role of speech and the exact connection between the sung sound and the spoken word are different in the different repertoires. The components of tone, texture, syllable-by-syllable intelligibility, and speech-like articulation all help to convey meaning, but each style of music prioritizes these components differently.

Many opera singers these days are producing "crossover" CDs with selections from both the classical and pop world. In many cases these performers' voices fit the pop style quite successfully. But do their voices still fit the classical style they believe they are coming from? Much of the time, I think not! The classical listener is being cheated. Singers who crossover from opera to musical theatre or pops need to stay there. The standard for musical theater would increase, but we would then have to determine what to do about opera . . .

When Wagner wanted Italianate performers to sing his operas, what really was he asking for? How many times do we have to hear "*mai piu*" to understand the text at a verbal level only to wonder what else the composer must have intended? The composer wanted the singer to caress the words, "spinning out" the most beautiful [u] vowel possible and melting the audience. The singer's concern, in addition to conveying the word itself, is for the beauty of the voice conveying the feeling of the words and phrases.

Legend has it that William Shakespeare yelled to his actors, "Words, words, words; too many words!" This unfortunately is now the state of opera. We are hearing words, but we are missing tone, tone, beautiful tone. We thirst for tone that is luscious and heartfelt, tones on which words ride like spinning air through the clouds, leaving the listener in an ecstasy of wonderment. These tones convey the true emotion of music.

Embedded in the word "emotion" we find another word "motion." When the sound is constricted, there is loss of fluidity, loss of that sense of motion. Tightness and stiffness dominate instead. We characterize performers who sing this way as having "*nothing to say with their voices*." How ironic this is because this singer is trying his or her darnedest to convey speech. Only the head voice allows a singer to produce that beautiful sound and clear text that conveys meaning and emotion.

Musicality

There are many stories of great singers discovered singing in the hills of Italy, or elsewhere, unlearned folk with no idea how to read music but possessing phenomenal voices. In our own time, great singers like Pavarotti, Freni, Manequerra, Bruscantini do not read music, yet they are the epitome of musicality. Where did they learn it?

First, let's distinguish between "musicality" and "musicianship." Musicianship Training might have been the name of a series of college courses. Score reading, rhythmic exercises, analysis and composition, as well as exposure to music literature, all have real value in developing musical sophistication. Musicality is different, though; it's a matter of understanding rhythmic ebb and flow, the fluidity of a line of music, the organic shape of a melody expressed in a performer's gestures. Audiences react to this musicality because these qualities mirror and evoke the shapes and gestures of "feelings" which we all have. The world of expression created by such musicality draws us to it.

This kind of musicality can be fostered but cannot be learned. It's not cognitive like learning music theory or history. It can't be learned, and more to the point, it does not have to be learned. **Musicality is inherent in the head voice because unlike chest voice or amplified music, head voice singing is innately beautiful and expressively free. It lacks constriction and excess pressure; there is no holding or bracing in the body; nothing pushes out or chokes off the breath. There is fluidity and freedom throughout the body and calmness in the mind. Any emotional, any musical impulse we have will be expressed effortlessly if we are singing in fully developed head voice.**

No one is devoid of emotional and musical impulses, but when we sing in head voice, we are musical. In my coaching sessions with students, eighty percent of our time is spent seeing to it that the vowels are in the head voice. When they are, singing language also falls into its proper place, subservient to the voice. Pushing is replaced by singing, even on the high notes.

If we do not sing in the head voice, musicality is a moot point. The constrictions in the body prohibit the freedom and fluidity of a musical gesture. The best we can do is fall back on **musicianship**, making sure we have all the double consonants and all the open or closed vowels textbook-perfect, driving harder for a *forte* and thinning down for a *piano*. Musicianship should serve musicality; by itself, it's a poor second.

When string players talk about making their instruments "sing," they are talking about the soaring, fluid freedom of the head voice. One of my students tells a story about herself before I met her; she was very interested in chamber music and spent most of her time with instrumentalists. As a voice student in college, she expressed an interest in joining a coaching group led by an eminent string player.

He welcomed her with open arms; she was the first voice student he had ever taken on, and he felt strongly that she was a musical person. He was looking forward to having a living example of that vocal legato and freedom in his class. She, however, was joining the class because she felt enormously frustrated; she felt unable to make her singing express her musicality. She wanted to learn how and thought he could help her. She sang for the teacher at the first session; he was crestfallen. He said, "Oh! I knew string players had to learn how to be free like singers, but I didn't realize that singers had to learn how to be free like other singers."

Together the string player/coach and the student spent hours and hours looking for ways to make the "musical gesture" she already felt inside. But she was singing with constriction and pressure throughout her entire vocal mechanism. She was standing in her own way, choking the breath, and she knew it. The coach couldn't help her and finally she told him: "I know how to make the music; I just don't know how to sing. When I figure that out, I'll be back." She had musicality, but because she wasn't able to sing with a head-dominant voice it wasn't realized. The absence of the head voice made a difference in her singing.

I've told her that in one sense I disagreed with what she had said at that time; her vision of what comes first was in error. As she is singing more purely and more reliably in the head voice, **there is no need to go back to make music with the new technique behind her**. The technique will lead her to discover her musicality. All she has to do is sing in her head voice and be true to herself. Instead of fighting her body, she will be able to focus on, foster, and develop the musical impulses she has. They will be heard.

I've said that no one is devoid of musical impulses, but some people have more to express than others do. Perhaps everyone has the same amount "to say," but some singers' temperament and personality are more flamboyant about saying it. Then too, an emotional connection between performer and listener depends partly on the temperament and openness of the listener. In this context perhaps we should examine the concepts of "beautiful," "musical," and "interesting."

Amusingly, these are the topics of many after-dinner arguments among aficionados of the voice. A recording of some famous singer is played. Half the listeners swoon; the other half agree the sound is beautiful but then respond after a few minutes that they are bored with it. The first group says they could listen to that sound forever, while the second group retorts that the first group must not be very interested in the music. The first group plays the recording again, pointing out all the musical gestures, shapes and colorations made by the performer. The second group merely reiterates that they are bored anyway.

Head voice singing is always beautiful and, because it is freely expressive of the individual performer, always musical. If a performance leaves half the room bored, it is a function of the competence of the singer. One thing is sure; any performer will certainly capture a larger audience if that performer sings with beauty and musicality, not with constriction and musicianship. All the greatest voices possessed the head voice. Many times, though, ego would infiltrate the organic process of singing trying to make one's voice larger than what Mother Nature provided. It's the difference between Kathleen Battle and Joan Sutherland, both of whom sing the same way, and other singers.

Carrying Power, Size, Volume, Intensity, Dynamics, and Pushing

One issue is just about every singer's main concern. It envelops a performer like a personal fog wherever that performer goes. It can be read like an LCD running across the performer's forehead. It's the question: "*Is my voice big enough???*"

Let's turn to the noted baritone Mack Harrell for the answer. He used to say, "*If the voice is beautiful enough, it is big enough.*" Given the emotion that singers understandably invest in the question, the solution to the riddle is startlingly simple.

There are a number of peripheral concepts that tend to muddle matters, so it might be useful to define some terms before continuing. When we use the word **intensity**, there are usually two possible contexts. One context is emotional intensity, which has nothing to do with the amount of noise a person is making and so doesn't belong in this section. The other meaning involves conceiving of **pitch**, **vowel**, and **intensity** and asking the body to produce those components. We are using the word synonymously with **volume**, and when we use the word **volume**, we are referring to the spectrum from *ppp* to *fff* within a performer's singing. For that usage we might as well consider the more academic word **dynamic**. **Intensity** and **volume** are not then terms that should be associated with a "**big voice**." We now should consider the terms **carrying power**, **size**, and **dynamics**.

Mack Harrell was really referring to carrying power. He was saying that if the voice is beautiful enough, it will be heard. The voice can only be truly beautiful—and can only be heard in the difficult circumstances of opera—through the head voice. Do you remember the following numbers? The head voice contains frequencies in the range of 3,000 cycles per second. The chest voice frequencies hover only in the range of 900 cps. The mean frequency of an orchestra is between 700-900 cps. Singers at the major opera houses of the world sing over a 100-piece orchestra and an 80-voice chorus in a 4,000-seat theater and they are heard without amplification. Most of today's performers are not singing pure head voice, but the head voice component of their singing most of the time makes them audible across the footlights. On Broadway, conversely, musical theater performers singing completely in chest voice must be miked, even in a 1,000-seat theater with a 16-piece band.

Carrying Power is a product of the head voice, but what about **size**. Some people use terms like "heavy" and "light" while others use "big" and "small." Most people mix the terminologies, using "light" and "big" because nobody wants to be told his or her voice is "small" or wants to hear about being "heavy."

The size of one's voice is whatever the head voice is. Kathleen Battle is different from Ruth Ann Swenson who is different from Joan Sutherland. The size of their voices determines in large measure the differences in their repertoire. But when each star sings, the size of her voice meets the needs of that repertoire. Why are they different? It's just part of who they are, like the color of their eyes. Perhaps the size of the body's skeletal frame has something to do with it. Joan Sutherland and Birgit Nilsson have big resonating chambers! This has nothing to do with weight. Greater poundage is beside the point, at least as far as the voice is concerned. Issues relating to emotional defenses and self-image are another matter, but from an acoustical point of view, fat doesn't vibrate very well . . . .

Of course, a performer wants his or her singing to be beautiful and expressive and most of all wants it to be heard. What is the point of all the struggling, dedication and passion, if nobody can hear the singing? In this context, the point to remember, again and again, is that it is not the size of the voice that determines whether or not one can be heard. Size and timbre may determine the roles one plays, but it does not determine whether the audience in the back of the house gets its money's worth. For that, what matters is **carrying power**. Head voice singing is not only beautiful and expressive, but because of the frequencies involved it also fills any theater.

I mentioned that the idea of a big voice was simple, but I know that it is a difficult point for many singers to trust at first. This is because there is so much confusion between **carrying power** and **size**. Most of us know someone who sounds like a bellowing bull up close but can't be heard in a large house, so we readily absorb the notion that sounding "big" or "loud" isn't quite enough. But most singing these days has such a big component of barking chest voice in it that the majority of coaches, audition committees, and conductors have come to expect it. They associate a "pushed" quality in the sound with loudness or carrying power. If they hear a singer in a small room with the ethereal, floating quality, the listener might assume that the voice will not be heard in the larger hall. Of course, they are wrong.

Singers themselves naturally are prey to the same concerns as coaches and promoters. This is true when singers are in the learning process. They are asked to give up the mechanism that they have come to associate with power and loudness. The head voice is there, ready to be uncovered, but at first it may be weak in proportion to how little it has been used. It takes time to find where the energy goes to strengthen the head voice, especially for those whose use of chest voice has been overwhelmingly dominant. It takes time to give up faith in the bellowing sound and put confidence in a different texture. This is especially the case for those performers with inherently lighter voices who are generally obsessed with having a voice "big enough" to carry. They are tempted to shout.

Here is a most interesting point about **carrying power**. A voice with terrific **carrying power** is not necessarily perceived as "loud" by somebody standing nearby. The "other side of the coin" is the bellowing tenor whose voice does not carry. It is an important lesson to learn to stand next to a short-range, loud singer and feel the blast, imagining the hair blown back tightly like in a cartoon. But it is a better, a more wonderful lesson to stand near a great singer, with carrying power, and discover that the sound is not at all overwhelming at close range. In fact, the voice sounds as "loud" near the source as it does many feet away.

Singers have a great deal of emotion invested in their art and a big part of their sense of self-worth invested in being heard. The desire to actively control this phenomenon is very strong. Because of those feelings, *resisting the temptation to push* is probably the single most difficult aspect of singing well.

A singer can feel control; he or she can sing in the head voice. Ironically, singing in the head voice requires resisting just that temptation to "muscle" the vocal mechanism to reach the goal of being heard. Especially in the western culture have we been taught to put our faith in the phenomenon of conscious control and to "try harder" for everything. Singing in the head voice, though, requires trust in the mechanisms beyond conscious control, a "*zen*-like" quality of trust that comes from "letting go." We'll return to this topic later in "Getting in the Zone."

Much has been said and written about another temptation that singers have trouble resisting: the desire to take on heavier roles than are appropriate for a performer's ability. What is this desire really about? It is fundamentally about the confusion between **size** and **carrying power**. If a performer sings in a production for a role that calls for a medium-sized voice, but then pushes a bit harder in the belief he or she can make the voice bigger, that performer is mistakenly associating the pushing with **carrying power**. It actually is a situation of **size**.

It's logical to think that by pushing a little harder one can ratchet the voice into a bigger size and be heard in a bigger role. We may have heard a dozen lectures about how dangerous "pushing" is, but resisting these warnings intellectually involves overcoming a powerful trio of forces: one, the desire every singer has to "blow people away" with sound; two, pressure from agents and managers who need a Wagner soprano or a Verdi mezzo; and three, the false logic of conscious control explained earlier.

With these three forces, the temptation to take on heavier roles is reduced to the desire to "push." Acquiescing to these forces means squeezing at the cords, adding breath pressure, "spreading" the vowels, and adding chest voice. It also means a shriller sound, less "spinning out," less floating, and less actual **carrying power**. Is that what a singer is really after?

Because of the cost to the vocal mechanism of sustaining that kind of tension, it can also mean a shorter professional life. Sometimes a singer consciously makes that choice, as Beverly Sills said she did in order to have the experience of singing specific repertoire. But if we make this choice, at least we should know what we are doing and do it consciously.

Even within a role that is appropriate for a singer's voice, the temptation to push arises time and again. Typically, this can happen when the orchestra is too loud, when the singer has pitches at the low end of his or her range, and when other singers on stage are out-screaming each other. Another instance of pushing occurs when there is little resonance or feedback in the performance space: outdoor concerts, and performances in "dead" halls. Unless and until we sing in pure head voice and trust it, we may begin to push under these circumstances, hoping to hear the echo that reassures us that we are "making enough noise." Unfortunately, pushing will not help us hear it; worse yet, the audience will hear even less.

TRUST IT: Singing in the head voice involves singing within a sensation of freedom and ease. You need think of little else.

Singing in the head voice will fill any theater regardless of the size of the voice. Does that mean that if we sing in head voice we will always be heard on every note? Does it mean that we will never, ever, be covered by the orchestra, the chorus, the wind and chatter at an outdoor performance, the high-pitched clink of glasses, and buzz of talk at a Pops concert?

NO!!! We can be covered by anything if we sing the wrong repertoire for our voice. In addition, we will be covered at the bottom of our range or when the orchestra is too loud.

I recently heard a Met telecast of *Arabella* with Kiri Te Kanawa—who sings with beautiful, spun, floating, expressive head voice—in the lead role. Early in the performance there was a duet between the lead and another soprano where the two vocal lines weave close to each other. In a telecast, of course, the sound coming from the TV set in the living room is electronically manipulated. It was clear, from my experience, that at the opera house, without the benefit of amplification, neither singer was being heard through considerable parts of the duet. The orchestra was just too loud.

What was interesting about the circumstances, though, was the difference in how the two singers handled the situation. The second soprano was pushing the voice considerably. Her concerns about being heard made her choose to be less sensitive to the dynamic variations in the music than she might have been. Her sound was strained, less fluid, and less beautiful than it could have been. What a pity for the telecast listeners. Te Kanawa resisted the temptation to fight the orchestra. She merely continued spinning that heady voice; she made sensuous music. Did she know she could not be heard in the house? Most likely, yes! She consciously chose beauty over competition and did so with all the benefits of the head voice.

I was asked to teach voice at the *Lee Strasberg Acting Institute and Actor's Studio*. I did this for three years and had some of the most interesting students, New York's finest young actors. I taught them in the same manner as I taught operatic voices. Lee Strasberg was a great lover of opera and appreciated this approach. The exercises were the same for both types of students; the acting students merely used the outcome in a different professional context. It became apparent that as these future actors' **head voices** improved for singing, so did their speaking voice. Often increasing the head voice in their singing resulted simply in discovering the head voice as a texture that could be used in any circumstance including acting.

As actors they were eager to explore textures, so they readily accepted a head voice technique. The head voice texture gave their speaking voices a rich velvety tone. The technique allowed them greater expressivity through more pitch variations and gave them a sense of freedom in the throat. In the past Strasberg had encouraged a method of speech similar to the "15 Rah" method. But using the head voice technique, these busy actors were delighted to discover that their voices did not tire as easily. Head voice aided the speaking voice, providing facility, health, and longevity to the performing voice.

The Music You Hear

In this age of rock-radio and mega-rock concerts, the rock gods of our society have become the icons of two generations. Children have been associating this texture of sound and this way of singing with success, strength, money, manliness or womanliness, and a super-person way of rising above the crowd's way of life. Little kids are singing along with the radio, imitating the male singer screaming and the female student belting. The more difficult it looks and feels, the more kids think it is the true conveyance of emotion. If a singer could spit blood, it would demonstrate a complete sacrifice for the art form. Today's young singer wants to emulate that, also.

Even Italy today is failing to produce the natural voice any more. Italian children are not imitating the adults; they are singing American rock. Singers adopt this way of thinking because, with the prevalence of amplification, they don't have to worry about being heard. Just turn up the volume! Because of this phenomenon "*Torna surriento*" is no longer of interest. This song and pieces like it were written as showpieces for the voice. But now the voice is only a tool for projecting words, conveying only those emotions that can be expressed by throaty, shouted sounds.

Sound and Self-Image

It's impossible to separate a performer's sound from the image that the performer has of him or herself. Each element reflects the other. How wonderful it must be to have an unconstricted voice which fits music written for one's voice category with all the notes of one's range being there, available in a free, open, and beautiful sound. Most of us, however, experience constriction, the constriction of the head voice by the muscles of the chest voice. This constriction brings tightness and tension into the larynx and the surrounding muscles. When the larynx is constricted, the entire respiratory system is also constricted. The constriction of the throat braces on other muscles, thereby also constricting down to the knees and up to the eyebrows.

When we deal with constriction as singers, our self image also suffers. Our basic instinct tells us that making music should not be tied up like this. We wonder what is wrong with us. Why are we so inadequate? To resolve these feelings of inadequacy, we take pills, go through hypnosis, drink alcohol, see a shrink, go through EST, and so forth. The solution is easier than these choices; just dump the constriction! We can become a new person by learning to sing in a way based on a positive self image of how we'd like to sing. This isn't the "snake oil" of Professor Harold Hill but rather the positive thinking of people like Dr. Maxwell Maltz in his book *Psychocybernetics*. Star athletes use it and so can star singers. Trust your instincts and your ability to change. Use your head; use your head voice!

EEEEHHHHH

Chapter 5
Vocal Constriction and Health

Physical Health: The Upper Respiratory System

Allergies, Asthma, Coughing, Reflux, Hyperactive Airways, Sinus Trouble . . .

The subject of health arises many times in the voice studio, for obvious reasons. Besides causing a specific performance to be canceled or complicating a particular rehearsal schedule, poor health can affect a singer in more habitual and more subtle ways. Simply stated, having less energy than one expects undermines confidence. Susceptibility to colds and viruses makes a singer worry about health for a performance before rehearsals get under way. The worrying itself can exacerbate a health problem.

Most singers pay a great deal of attention to how their health affects their singing. I propose some attention to the reverse: *How does our singing affect our health?*

The memoirs of many old time singers remind us that worries about "catching cold" have always been part of every singer's baggage. In this generation, however, we seem to be dealing more and more with *chronic* conditions. Listen to any backstage conversation and we likely will hear choruses of talk about how singers are medicating themselves to cope, not with a specific cold or flu, but with the upper respiratory problems they encounter in everyday life.

Allergies and sensitivities to chemicals around us are both more common and more often recognized than ever before, and many singers are paying attention to the role they can play in vocal health. But first consider the false connections made between one's singing and one's upper respiratory health.

One connection, though it may be painful to consider, is really a ruse. How often has a performer incorrectly excused poor singing on poor health? Health problems may be very real. But should the idea that health problems cause vocal problems prevent a performer from looking more closely at vocal techniques? Some performers are satisfied blaming less than stellar singing on bad health. They need to be open to other considerations and investigate technique, also. Another connection, not so erroneous, may seem even more radical, but I have seen it borne out again and again. Reverse the previous argument: *Is poor singing the cause of one's poor health?*

Let's remember the main thesis of this book: *Chest voice singing is constricted singing; head voice singing is free and unconstricted.* The breathing musculature in chest voice singing is braced against tightly held vocal folds. There is tension and contortion in the entire respiratory tract, in the larynx, the pharynx, the back of the tongue, the soft palate. . . . The point of this litany is that this kind of tension means we are singing less beautifully than we could. It also means we are less comfortable than we could be. That is a pity but also truly unhealthy! Incorrect technique causes the unacceptable vocal product; it also causes bad health.

Distortion and tensions can cause problems strictly from a mechanical point of view. Things are rubbing against each other that shouldn't be; things are stretched that shouldn't be; things are knotted up that shouldn't be. Particularly bad is the internal stress placed on a muscular mechanism that receives simultaneously but contradictory instructions to be taut and yet move. The vocal cords are being asked to resist the air flow, and yet are taking the friction and pressure of an air flow forceful enough to bend them anyway. These factors apply stress that can lead to later health issues.

Unnecessarily tense and constricted musculature, anywhere in the body, means occluded blood flow and slower elimination of chemical waste products. The areas of the body involved in singing include mucous membranes, which can be particularly sensitive to both mechanical irritation and the build up of toxins. A membrane's protective reaction is to produce phlegm, but the phlegm itself can act as an irritant. For many people this perpetuates a cycle that looks, feels, and sounds very much like one of several very common upper respiratory problems, involving chronically thickened, phlegmy vocal cords, a chronic "tickle" and cough, and so forth.

Are all singers wrong who say their phlegm, cough, and thickened cords are allergy-related? Certainly not! Irritants are very real. Who can afford to deal with mechanical irritation and poor fluid exchange on top of allergy-related irritants?

Suppose a performer has excess stomach acid together with reflux, or a food intolerance that causes phlegm production in the upper respiratory tract. Either of these problems can set off a cough. How costly that cough is depends partly on whether or not it continues chronically, causing enough mechanical irritation to make the respiratory tract produce a cushion of phlegm. How costly that phlegm is, depends on whether or not it is irritating enough to trigger coughing itself and fuel the vicious cycle. Now suppose that this person is a singer whose way of singing involves constriction. The constriction causes mechanical irritation just at the site that can least afford any irritation.

Adding insult to injury, the effort to continue singing under these conditions typically involves two possible reactions. One is an effort to compensate for the problem. Unfortunately, the attempt will probably, if not definitely, cause a new set of problems. An analogy is someone who hurts a foot and then shifts his or her weight unevenly to avoid the pain, ultimately causing back problems from the asymmetrical load on the joints. When a singer tries to compensate for the biochemical and mechanical irritation with the vocal mechanism, damaging consequences become even more likely. The entire mechanism is so delicate and there is no gross musculature that can be utilized to relieve the burden.

The other result of singing under these conditions involves troubled vocal cords. Under too much pressure or when abraded by too much friction, the cords thicken to protect themselves. They become engorged with fluid. Unfortunately, thick cords do not vibrate as easily as thin ones. Moreover, it is more difficult to bring the edges of the vocal cords together. This means that a singer with this condition must move the cords more forcefully to make them function and must blow air between them more strenuously to make them buzz. This is not just compensation, not just one of several possible ways to avoid the problem. It is actually a direct consequence necessitated by the condition of the cords. We might ask what is the upshot of this condition and the resultant action? The answer is that more muscularity and greater pressure must be applied, i.e., further constriction. Now the problem is compounded: constriction caused by poor vocal technique and constriction caused by "bad" health.

I have had many students suffering from chronic respiratory problems. They came ostensibly for lessons to help their voices, not their health, but they expressed painful frustration concerning how those health problems had complicated their singing. I did not attempt to solve those problems; we worked on vocal technique. In each case I enjoyed watching the severity of those health symptoms diminish as they learned to sing more and more purely with the head voice.

These singers were amazed to discover that old problems were easily surmounted. Some, incapacitated in past years during pollen season, discovered that now they were able to work less encumbered. They may continue to experience allergy symptoms and even discomfort, but it needn't fundamentally interfere with their singing any more. Their incorrect singing technique, now changed to the head voice texture, no longer exacerbated the health problem but made the problem manageable.

I have seen and experienced myself the same dynamics between health and singing when the problem is an episode of illness such as a viral or bacterial infection. Sometimes, of course, it is impossible to continue singing when an infection takes hold in the upper respiratory system and the cords are thickened; it is even damaging to try singing. Compared to performers whose vocal technique would add irritation and phlegm of its own, those singers whose technique doesn't compound the situation can "afford" to become much sicker before the illness overcomes sound.

In my own life and in my studio, I have seen demonstrated time and time again a critical relationship between the vocal mechanism of choice and a singer's upper respiratory system. It has become abundantly clear that the constrictions and tensions of chest voice production *add* terribly to the list of mechanical and chemical irritations with which the upper respiratory system must deal. Singing in the head voice never exacerbates those *added* irritations and may actually help reduce them.

Physical Health: Body Use

Restlessness, Knotted Muscles, Labored Breathing . . .

Not only can poor sound production lead to health issues, but it also can lead to other physical discomforts. The body does its best to give us what we want. If we ask our bodies to produce a throaty, shrill, or barking sound with great heaves of pressurized air, our body will give it to us even if it has to squeeze and contort to oblige. But this book concerns the production of velvety, beautiful, fluid, musical, expressive vocal sound. We cannot produce such a sound with a tense, constricted, overly muscular, pressurized instrument.

Consider also the issue of stage presence and health. Besides the specific phenomenon of gorgeous sound production, a performer should be aware of how vocal and total physical health affect the way he or she is seen on the stage. Performers with great stage presence whether as actor, dancer, clown, or singer are noteworthy for their ability **to be still**. They are able to remain **still** in an easeful, graceful, fluid way, yet charged with energy. Constriction and tension anywhere in the body is absolutely destructive to that state. Until vocal problems became too difficult to mask, Maria Callas was noted for her ability to remain still and display outstanding stage presence. All the great singers possess this attribute; they eliminate tension in the body.

Wieland Wagner once was speaking to Birgit Nilsson about movement and acting. He told her: "It's silly to run around, making ridiculous gestures, and contorting your face like a wounded animal. You cannot compete with Wagner's music. Learn how to be still and express your feelings with simplicity and honesty." What a wonderful, succinct statement on movement, singing, and acting. Let that be the watch-word; less really is more and less reduces constriction.

Typically, people are not aware of the habits of their body, nor how far from a balanced state it can get. Ingrained habits, both good and bad, can go unnoticed, and we may not consciously remember what it feels like to be free of excess physical tension while singing. Many of my students are devotees of various disciplines that assist in rediscovering freedom of movement and that also sensitize one to the concept of **body use**. The Alexander Technique, *Feldenkrais*, yoga, and tai chi are just a few systems they have mentioned. For good singing and increased comfort, flexibility and efficient use of the body are certainly not values to be discouraged.

These disciplines, though, are not at the heart of solving problems for singers. Poor **body use** habits can have a purely mechanical or emotional source which perhaps can be addressed by body/mind disciplines. My job as a voice teacher forces me to face the vocal phenomena, not only the vocal "consequences" of poor body use but also the vocal "source" of this problem.

Throughout this book I've pointed out links between singing and other conscious, emotional, or physical issues. In each case, I also find myself trying to find the root cause of a singing problem, asking, **"Which comes first?"** Can one "fix" constricted singing simply by "fixing" constricted **body use**? The answer is "No!" Solving incorrect body use alone will not solve constriction and tension of the vocal mechanism. In this context, good singing comes before "body use." What about the variant question: can one "fix" constricted body use without "fixing" constricted singing? Again, "No!"

F.M. Alexander (the Alexander Technique) was interested in the study of **body use**. In doing so, he discovered a wealth of information about the ways poor **body use** can interfere with vocal production. Although he focused entirely on body issues as the source of health and vocal problems, Alexander also discovered how difficult it can be to break habits of poor **body use**. He based a major part of his teaching on the idea that one must learn to avoid sending the wrong instructions to the body before one can possibly be successful sending the right instructions about **body use**. To the question of *which comes first*, Alexander's answer was "the body."

It's important to note that Alexander was originally an orator, not a singer. His perspective concerned the spoken word and not the sung word. He wanted to be heard and understood as an actor, obsessed only with the spoken sound. He was not, like an opera singer, concerned with the vocal and tonal quality of the sound. He found it was difficult to inhibit constricting body habits and so was essentially willing to accept whatever sound was produced when he tried. A singer is generally committed to the quality of sound, even though struggling against poor **body use** habits. For singers it is imperative to commit to the right quality of sound and to utilize the best vocal technique to produce that sound.

The command our brain issues to our vocal mechanism always takes precedence. If the sound we ask the body to make is a pressurized sound, the body will oblige in spite of other instructions to remain fluid. We know the two choices for a singer concerning vocal production (chest-dominated voice or head voice), but it is practically impossible to protect the vocal mechanism from the effects of tension elsewhere in the body. This condition, or contradiction, sometimes automatically controls our choosing. Conversely, tension in the vocal mechanism means tension throughout the face, neck, and torso. In choosing a constricted, pressurized, chest voice texture, we are choosing a state of unnecessary discomfort for the whole body. And so, our choice of vocal production supersedes **body use**.

Marked increase in both upper respiratory health and general physical comfort and poise are bonuses of head voice singing! These bonuses certainly create a happier bunch of people than those performers complaining backstage about their allergies, aches, and pains. Being happier, calmer, more confident, more secure, and more comfortable inhabiting our tension-free bodies is the juncture where physical health meets mental health.

Mental Health

Anxiety, Irritability, Lack of Confidence, "Nerves" on and off the stage . . .

Performers are not known for being a particularly stable, calm, easy-going bunch of people. On stage we put much of ourselves at stake, completely unprotected and vulnerable. The sense, the identity of who we are is very much tied to how successful we are on stage. Some of us measure that success by applause or contracts; some of us measure it against an internal standard which may be even more difficult to meet.

We've dealt with purely physical problems; ultimately, however, the physical issues do link with mental ones and vice versa. The way we used the word "feel" earlier illustrates this relationship rather well. Note the double meaning of the word "feel." *I feel sick/achy/tight* and *I feel insecure/worried/ sad.* Both sentences make good us of the word "feel" but each reveals two different perspectives. The first suggests a physical frame of reference; the latter suggests a psychological one. The total organism of body and mind responds as a whole to any given demand; separating and differentiating can be difficult. Demands on the body will cause both a physiological and psychological reaction. These demands can be called **stressors** and they can influence the mind, or the body, or both.

"**Stress**" is a loaded word, like the word "**tension**." On the one hand, these words denote something straightforward and objective. Without necessary muscle tension, our bodies would simply collapse in a heap; that's an objective use. The use of the word "**stressor**" in this context simply refers to the fact that each demand made upon the muscular system is not a neutral event; it has an effect. It requires a change of the status quo; that's normal. We tend to take "necessary" tension and the phenomenons of basic stress for granted, however, and use these words instead to connote **extra** tension and **too much** stress. The words immediately acquire a negative connotation. Just thinking about them can bring on a sense of anxiety.

But used in a context that embraces negative connotation, stress is not synonymous with **anxiety**. Stress in this context is more correctly divided into **anxi-**

ety and **tension**. **Anxiety** is the stress reaction of the mind—a psychological response; **tension** is the stress reaction of the body—a physical response. Both elements act together; neither can be separated from the other. This is why anxiety mushrooms like an atomic bomb when a singer becomes increasingly concerned about his or her performance; anxiety begins translating itself into physical tension.

How often, how prolonged, and how paralyzing the anxiety is will depend on the psychological strength the performer possesses: how vulnerable to anxiety is the performer; how much anxiety can he or she take before becoming "tied up in knots"? The degree to which anxiety develops also depends on how tense the body is initially and how much tension a correct or incorrect way of singing affects the total system.

As a professional singer and as a teacher I have seen undue stress—both **tension** and **anxiety**—in a thousand forms. There are singers who carry stress with them all day, who have come to believe that living in a state of constant insecurity, irritability, and "nerves" comes with the job and is normal. Sadly, they think it is *just the way they are*. They accept this plight as part of a routine day but tension and anxiety increases especially on days of high drama. Auditions and opening nights stand out as something special for just about every singer; so do competitions, first rehearsals in front of colleagues, and final rehearsals with the orchestra. Many singers simply cannot sing opening nights, orchestral rehearsals, or *sitzprobes*; they choke. One quite famous dramatic soprano frequently choked on these occasions and for a time stopped singing. Upon her return, her comeback at the Met, the administration went to the orchestral rehearsal to hear her; she choked.

Robert Triplett in his book *Stagefright: Letting it Work for You* gives us a comprehensive description of just how all-encompassing an event can be when we go into a "flight or fight" reaction to the circumstances. He also makes it very clear that there is no such thing as a purely physical or purely emotional event.

> A dramatic shift of body energies takes place to prepare for protective action, thus producing an array of physical symptoms. The muscles throughout the body contract, priming it to spring with a burst of energy (either to flee or fight). In this contraction, the neck muscles pull the head down and the shoulders up, while the back muscles drive the spine into a concave curve. This in turn retracts the pelvis, pulling the genitals up in a vestigial protection reaction. The blood vessels constrict and the blood pressure elevates, heating up the entire mechanism. In an effort to cool the system down perspiration is released. But since the blood is not flowing freely through the constricted vessels, especially the extremities, the sweat is cold. Nevertheless, the heart works overtime to get blood to these areas and in so doing causes the face to become flushed. . . . The need for oxygen increases as does our breathing rate but, with the diaphragm muscles shortened, our breaths are shallow and irregular. Eyesight is also distorted. Our pupils dilate to get a broader visual perspective, but

> this causes vision to be unfocused. . . . To compound the entire problem, brain-wave frequency increases. The individual feels overwhelmed and confused, as if too many data are coming into the head. . . . Increased brain-wave activity changes the entire sense of timing and pacing, so that a variety of miscalculations are likely to surface.

Many times singers who are sick and tired of living with anxiety—on or off the stage—focus on the anxiety itself as their problem. They think of it as a neurosis and look for help. They go for speech therapy, take prescribed drugs, or indulge in self-medication, taking as gospel everybody's cure-all like snake-oil. This process fills the pocket of psychiatrists, therapists, throat doctors, and pharmaceutical companies but does not strike at the root cause, **stress**—both anxiety and tension.

A special word at this point needs to be proffered about anxiety-lessening drugs and alcohol. These "chemicals" work by depressing the entire central nervous system. The resulting sedative effects include sleepiness, impaired fine-muscle coordination, and interference with mental and physical perception of the body, the vocal instrument, and the performance, as well as dependency both physically and psychologically. In addition to these disadvantages, alcohol is a vasodilator; its use can lead to bruising of the vocal cords and increased mucous production. It's true that Lauritz Melchior drank a bottle of red wine almost every night before he sang . . . not to mention the alcoholic exploits of Jussi Bjoerling and Kirsten Flagstadt, but their success in spite of the self-abuse is the exception. For most of us, drugs and alcohol don't mix with the demands of an operatic career.

Another popular remedy in the treatment of stage fright is B-adrinoceptor antagonists, otherwise known as beta-blockers. These drugs suppress the physical symptoms of stage fright without the sedative effects of tranquilizers or alcohol; they block the overwhelming rush of adrenaline and energy from that part of the nervous system that responds to a perceived threat. This means the drug checks those physical responses such as tremor, rapid heart beat, and high blood pressure without affecting the entire nervous system. However, many times the anxiety of stage fright remains even though the physical symptoms are gone. The most dangerous potential side-effect of beta-blockers is asthma or an asthma attack which may be particularly severe in those already predisposed to asthma. Depression, short-term memory loss, and disorientation have also been noted as side effects of beta-blockers.

Sataloff and Robert put it perfectly in their book *Stress in Singers*:

> If a singer has such severe stage fright that [he or she is] unable to perform without the help of an ingested substance, his underlying problem should be treated, not masked with drugs. We must remember in these circumstances that we are dealing with a person who requires a drug to perform the daily activities of his chosen profession.

Needing to be drugged to pursue one's vocation. . . . "Choking" just at a critical moment . . . Throwing up before performances. . . . What is going on here? "I'm just nervous," describes the outcome of a problem, not the problem itself. To get at the problem itself, we must address the question of why someone is nervous in the first place.

Is nervousness really first and foremost a question of "emotional baggage"? I don't think so. *Everybody* has emotional baggage. *Everybody* has voices in or her head making judgments. *Everybody* has a lot at stake in his or her chosen vocation. *All* performers are vulnerable onstage. So why do different singers suffer in varying degrees from anxiety? Why do some singers choke and others don't? Individual temperament—difficult if not impossible to change—certainly accounts for some of the differing reactions to anxiety. For example, Vladimir Horowitz' legendary stage fright was a consequence of pure shyness—not insecure playing, not a lack of confidence from limited success as a performer. Talk therapy might provide relief from some of the emotional baggage, but it's not a permanent solution to anxiety.

When voices inside our heads are overwhelmingly loud and most critically reflect memories of *other people*, such as parents, teachers, childhood authority figures, it is immensely important to identify, demystify and shush these harbingers. The real dividing line in dealing with this form of stress—anxiety (stage fright)—is between **performers who trust their voices** and those who don't. The core of most singers' nervousness is frequently **insecure singing**. Singing securely through proper vocal technique will see the elimination of the signs of stress—tension and anxiety.

Why do I see **insecure singing** at the heart of the matter of stress? If we feel that we must physically do this or that before the voice can work properly . . . what happens if we don't or can't produce that physical change? If we feel comfortable only when it isn't allergy season . . . what do we do if it is allergy time? If we think that we should have a fluid breathing mechanism but it's tight as a drum . . . what happens when we try unsuccessfully to prepare for a long phrase? If we're not sure whether our voice will carry but we know we shouldn't push . . . what happens if we fail to properly deal with the conflicted energy of these two states? In rehearsal or in performance we constantly feel at the mercy of hopelessly contradictory forces and factors outside our control. And this lack of control is the root of **insecure singing**, the cause of performance anxiety, stress. Conflict and powerlessness put us in a position of vulnerability. These are the two most powerful producers of anxiety in human experience.

Perhaps even worse is this scenario. What if in our heart of hearts we are unsatisfied with how we sound and how our body feels? As we stand there singing, we think to ourselves consciously or subconsciously, *"My body is tense and my sound is thin and edgy, or thick and mushy. . . . I'm going to sing anyway because I really want to. But oh how I wish the physical situation were better, how I wish I had taken a better breath, what do I do with my hands, is my face expressive enough, and I hope these strangers don't notice."*

When the audition is over and we get the part in spite of it all, we relax a bit. *"The scam worked!"* we think. But the first orchestral rehearsal presents a whole new group of strangers to scam—colleagues at that—and opening night yet another crisis. The internal monologue continues: *"Will they hear that my voice is not beautiful, and will they sense how effortful my singing is? When will I be found out?"*

In everyday life we all are probably people of integrity; but on stage as performers our body is attempting to present an image of success, attempting to pull another scam on strangers. This conflict takes a terrible toll. Our training, our experience, our scamming tells us we need to display a palpable attitude of confidence; we think that we are expected to radiate love for our own voice as well as for the art of singing and the many works we perform. It works for a few. Some singers love their voices in spite of sounding ghastly; these performers often find work on the strength of their own ego-driven illusions. That's a new level of scam, fooling oneself. I often wonder if such people really believe their own press.

The other level of scam is perhaps more common; it involves singers who are secretly frustrated with their voices but find work because—everything being relative—they sound "OK." If they are able to project the image of loving their voices when they really don't, the attitude in the industry is *so much the better*. This was a position I myself could never accept. As a singer I couldn't morally accept the deception; I wanted to help others avoid the predicament and I wanted to create a cleaner environment for quality singing. Experimenting and suffering at the hands of some, I finally realized the real value of quality singing through the head voice. It reduces stress; it eliminates pressurized singing; it produces a far more beautiful and velvety sound.

The fear of being *found out* is quite basic because singing is a very personal act. Many singers, suffering from the dissatisfactions and discomforts of an insecure voice, feel that how they sing is not their real voice. Their "real selves" are aching to be heard through a voice they have not yet found. The performer's monologue continues: *"Will they know that this isn't really my voice but just the best I can do right now? When will 'right now' be over and my real musical self be able to emerge? What on earth should I do to make that happen?"*

The answer to these questions lies in learning how to sing in a way that does not fuel a continuing, vicious cycle of anxiety-begetting tension and tension-begetting anxiety. We must learn how to sing in a way that does not require pushing, pulling, straining, and forcing. As long as there is conflicting muscularity in our singing, we are open to all of the stresses we hate: vulnerability, conflicts, contradictions, a sense of powerlessness, and a secret dislike of our own voice.

Chest-dominated singing is muscular and pressurized. It feeds into the vicious cycles of anxiety and tension, of secrecy and disapproval. Head voice singing narrates another story altogether. Physically, it requires much less effort; emotionally, it is much more satisfying. Ironically, though, head voice singing is effortless, yet difficult. Once learned, this vocal technique makes singing easier, but unfortunately, it is difficult to hand over control of the singing process to the reflexive self. As long as we use the feelings of pushing here, pulling there, squeezing this, and holding that in order to feel in control, singing in the head voice will remain foreign and difficult to achieve. This is one of several reasons that head-voice dominated singing is so rare. It's also one of the reasons that head voice singing is so wonderful; it is a profound relief to a singer to experience this quality of *letting go*.

Audiences hear this effortless sound in head voice singing and sense the ease of performance with this technique; they are transported by it to a different level of appreciation. We'll hear more about this in the chapter **Getting in the Zone**. I introduce it here because I do not want to imply that all we have to do is snap our fingers or sign up for one workshop and we'll magically understand and achieve the head voice quality of production. I do want to suggest, however, that in singing, as in just about every other human endeavor, gritting our teeth and *trying harder to get it right* never breaks the vicious cycles of stress. Both body and mind clench tighter and tighter. Mental and physical health are jeopardized and each in turn jeopardizes the other.

Look at the word *Dis-ease*. The overriding experience of singing should be *easefulness*. If *easefulness* is not our experience, we should be thoughtful and careful about how we pinpoint a vocal problem. One corollary to the effort to control is the tendency to blame. We must be wary of leaping to the conclusion that our voice is the problem, or our temperament is the problem, or thinking it is just the way we are. Blaming ourselves injudiciously will only cause the stress cycle to tighten. Of course, there is a long list of issues we can blame that may not be so aggravating but aren't helpful either: our parents, our allergies, or a cough, nerves, our spouse or old childhood expectations, our body type or our reaction to smog, fluorescent lights, etc. . . . Constrictive behavior learned and habitualized is the root culprit against quality singing. When underlying faulty vocal production is corrected and the performer understands and appreciates the beautiful and efficient voice he or she has developed, most of the negative feedback will stop and the singer will begin building a repertoire of success experiences.

Let two sopranos, at different stages of their career, reveal what it can be like.

> **Leontyne Price**: *I did something right. I took care of the most extraordinary thing I have—my voice. And, I think I've had one of the most beautiful lyric soprano voices I've ever heard. I'm mad about my voice. It was gorgeous. I loved it so much that from time to time I used to take out one of my best crystal glasses, sip a little champagne, and toast it.*

Lauren Flanigan is one of the stars of the opera world, and I'm fortunate to say for 14 years one of my students. She has become so recognized as a singer that composer Philip Glass wrote a symphony for her. Lauren premiered the work in Germany with the Linz Philharmonic with Rodney Russell Bennett conducting; and just recently she performed the New York premier of the work with the same orchestra. The piece is both beautiful and exciting and Lauren sang like a dream—55 minutes of constant singing. The composition hovered around high G and high C with many big dramatic moments. Lauren sang with such ease and beauty that I really could not believe it. For the premier and recording of this work, she said she was tired and did not feel great about the singing. But not here; the performance was fantastic! When it was over, I went backstage to meet and congratulate Lauren. She grabbed me by one hand and introduced me to everyone as "my teacher, the person who gave me my **head voice** which allowed me to sing this piece tonight." It is amazing what a difference singing can make with the use of the head voice—effortless production, excellent resonance, and that rich velvety texture. The power of the head voice is superior to any other way of singing.

Part 2: Getting There

"It always has been thought that Italian has five 'pure' vowels: 'ah, eh, ee, oh, oo,' but actually this has not been true in singing for generations. In 1932 Pertille dictated a singing method, *Metodo di Canto*, [which] codified what by then had become standard practice for men: 'ah' should be blended with 'oh.' 'Oh' should sound like 'oh,' 'ee' should sound like 'ih,' 'eh' should be blended with 'oo,' 'oo' should be blended with 'oh.' He said that in singing with this approach, the five vowels, which in speaking are dissimilar, come to resemble one another. . . . Like Pertile, Del Monaco and Corelli darkened 'ah, ee, and eh.' But unlike Pertile they sang 'oo' as 'oo.' "

Stefan Zucker, "Aureliano Pertile on Vowels," Bel Canto Society, June 2006

Chapter 6
Bel Canto and Head Voice: *What Happened?*

Great Singers

Pavarotti and Freni walked out of the hills of Modena, Italy, right onto the stage of La Scala, not even knowing how to read music. Tucker, Merrill, Price, Pinza, Nilsson, Caballe, and Callas began singing and their professional training in their late teens; their voices were developed as major operatic singers. What allows this to happen to some? There is no answer to this question beyond "fates fortune." But if it happens to as many performers as it does, then the rest of us must not be as far off as we think.

It is worth noting what these performers themselves say about the voice and about vocal technique. Jerome Hines in his book *Great Singers on Great Singing* reveals some interesting comments made by these singers:

> **Corelli**—If you feel the voice striking in the mask, you know that the voice and throat are free.
>
> **Horne**—I feel my whole concentration is coming out here in the front . . . in the mask.
>
> **Ponselle**—You use the mask for placement.
>
> **Pavarotti**—For me the position is always high . . . even when I sing low notes.
>
> **Sutherland**—One feels as if the sound were being projected against the front of the hard palate.

> **Nilsson**—I try to place the voice as far in front as possible . . . in the mask . . . without getting nasal. When I feel that the voice just bangs in the head, then I know it is in place.

The really great singers never speak of the voice in terms of their throats because they "feel" nothing there. What they talk about is secondary resonance, the resonance that excites small bones and cartilage in the head. When a singer talks about "feeling" a sensation in the throat, we can be assured that he or she is not "feeling" any sensation in the head and is not producing the frequencies needed for that sensation to be there. It also means that the singer is not among the ranks of the truly great singers.

An audience attending the performance of a great singer speaks of being privileged to have been a part of the occasion. Part of this is a celebrity effect, but if a performer sings exceptionally well, the event takes on legendary proportions—the Lisbon *Traviata*, Rio's *Turandot*, Flagstaad's Met Debut, Nilsson's *Electra*, Ring Cycle, and *Turandot*, etc.

What happens to make these events magical, electrifying, unforgettable experiences? It is **sound**, free beautiful sound! It is sound produced so freely and efficiently that every space in the theatre is resounding with the incredible span of frequencies. It is the "singer's frequency" (3000cps) that is most prominent amidst all those sounds. Once again, this frequency can only be produced when the larynx is in equilibrium. Not only is there balance with no stress or pressure but it is tuned to the magic number (3000cps).

The human ear canal, according to the book *The Human Body* (Bell Laboratory), is also tuned to this frequency, so the audience is able to hear it above the orchestral range and is able to feel it. An orchestra can never block our enjoyment of great singers. Their sound can soar over a large orchestra with a 100-voice chorus. We are bathed in the sound; it many times connects us with primal as well as aesthetic feelings. We may be moved to cry when this connection is made. But as soon as there is constriction, the larynx moves and closes, the frequency changes, and this magical experience is gone.

What are we talking about? We are referring to **head voice** production and technique. That's the difference between an average voice and a great voice.

Naming the Phenomenon

What is it that we are actually talking about when referring to muscular singing on the one hand or reflexive movement on the other? We are referring to a condition where the voice sings but the body does not consciously respond. This takes place when singing is performed without movement of the larynx. This is also a good definition of the head-voice technique of singing.

When the larynx moves, it does so because of the action of a group of muscles that move it. These muscles are creators of a sound we know as chest voice or chest register. Chest voice is the mixture of the *falsetto* and chest register, but it is being strongly dominated by the chest. Chest register is an independent register, functioning in most people's voices at the very bottom of the range. When the voice is made up of a *falsetto*-dominated registration, the texture is quite different. The "feeling" associated with the production of both sounds is also quite different.

When the singing voice is produced without laryngeal movement, there is no feeling in the larynx. This phenomenon occurs because there are no proprioceptive nerves that deal with internal laryngeal movement, only receptors to "pick up on" external movement. Logically, when there is no proprioceptive nerve feedback, there can be no "feeling." This is what we refer to when we speak of a singer possessing a great natural voice. This also helps us discern how much a singer who has sung brilliantly throughout his or her whole career knows about the actual process of singing.

Bel Canto in History

The *Bel Canto* Period of the 18th to mid 19th century was an age of singing when beauty and purity of sound were given high priority in the standard of acceptable singing. There is only speculation as to how this period began, but surely it coincided with the moment singers began to use their voices in a more sophisticated manner, emphasizing beauty of line and tone. Composers in turn wrote for these voices, encouraging more singing in this manner. Voice teachers eventually began to teach these principles.

As Edmund J. Myer states in his *Position and Action in Singing*:

> Nature was the great teacher and not man. Man when he bases his teaching upon his own ideas of voice is too artificial: hence artificiality. Witness the many ridiculous things singers are taught to do. With such, the effort to make the voice, to compel it, instead of allow it. Nature teaches differently. The voice is in Nature, and by a study of Nature and Nature's laws the voice is allowed to develop, is allowed or induced to reveal itself instead of being made or forced.

For the *Bel Canto* period to evolve, a few generations of singers had to be working with their instruments on the basis of a principle like Myer's, striving for a "natural" production of the singing voice. Teachers and vocal performers of this period through analysis and trial and error must have discovered what the "seed" of singing was and realized that they already had it within themselves, needing only to nurture it. Since then an essential misunderstanding of that "seed" has led many voice teachers down the wrong path for decades. Very few in recent generations have discovered the true essence of *bel canto* singing and acted upon it in their methods of instruction.

What Happened?

So, what happened that caused us to stray from beautiful, natural singing? In one word, the **laryngoscope**! At the turn of the 20th century, the noted voice teacher Manuel Garcia put a small-mirrored instrument in the back of the throat and changed the world of singing. *Voila!*—there they were—two little bands only 5/8ths of an inch in length and vibrating away. All of a sudden, the source of quality vocal production shifted and it was now thought to originate in the throat. If vocal sound was no longer in the head or the chest but in the throat, teachers concluded, then the throat was where we should "feel" it.

Interestingly, since this great misdirection, the word "throaty" with its negative connotation is no longer used to describe singing. Now every voice student is being taught that the throat is where everyone should be singing. Because the word evokes a negative image, describing one's sound as "throaty" must be avoided.

With this shift of awareness and focus to the throat, every aspect of the voice changed: teaching, singing, coaching, diction, the very concept of musicality. With "throaty" singing, words could now be heard as if **SPOKEN**. Now every open and closed vowel, every double consonant, and nasalized vowel took on a life of its own, a new importance, a new "something" for which we now could get a college degree.

One serious disadvantage developed from this shift. Because singing was now "throaty," it could no longer be truly *legato*. Now singers were taught and coached to sing *legato* in an unnatural way. The quality of sound they produced was not natural, involving greater contortions, and only yielding more stress to the vocal instrument and the body in general. To overcome this and still sing successfully was a phenomenon only achieved by exceptionally good singers who were "blessed." True *legato* can only be achieved through the head voice; its effortless and stressless production is truly natural singing. If employed correctly this natural phenomenon is achievable by any singer, including those less "blessed."

My student Lauren Flanigan recently sang Verdi's *I Lombardi* at the Met with Luciano Pavarotti, James Levine conducting. After one of the performances, Levine congratulated me and told me that Lauren sang like one of the great *Bel Canto* divas. This was the best compliment anyone could have given me and certainly is a ringing endorsement for a return to head-voice dominated singing in the opera world and in all singing.

Chapter 7
The *Passaggio*:
To What? From What?

Oh, that dreadful word "*passaggio*"! It is every singer's source of confusion: Do I have one? Should I have one? How many should I have? Is it too high or too low? Why?

Italian voice teachers frequently referred to the *passaggio* as the "bridge of sorrow," and said that every singer had one. Many teachers taught that if a singer **sang through the *passaggio*** correctly, he or she was on track with the voice. Many teachers currently, though, teach that there is no such thing as a *passaggio* and that a seamless voice should not have any kind of passage or break in it. These teachers claim, "Every note is its own register," "there are no registers," or "the voice has five registers," etc. What really is going on here; does it really need to be a sorrowful experience?

When I was 27 and singing professionally, I did not really understand the *passaggio*. I was singing with Jose Carerras, the international tenor. We were preparing for a production of *Lucrezia Borgia* with the Dallas Opera. Every day he would go on and on that his entrance line on an F-natural was so high. He couldn't understand, he would say, why Donizetti would compose in such a way. Of course, every time Carerras sang the line, it sounded absolutely gorgeous despite his protestations. A pirated recording of that production proves how exciting the performances were even though a challenge to the *passaggio* of one of the great tenors of opera.

This response to the *passaggio* is not an uncommon event. Alfredo Krause responded the same way. F-natural was a note that he always had to think about in terms of where the line was headed and what vowel he was singing. Luciano Pavarotti has said many times in Master Classes that he never sings the F-natural "open." He's also said that a singer who sings "too open" through the *passaggio* risks loosing his high notes, or at least making them much more difficult to achieve. For him, use of the word "open" implies a negative context. A serious point of irony, though, is that most of us struggle our whole lives to sing "open." That implies freedom from constriction in the larynx. So why is open here a negative? Consider that we can also say that someone sings "too open" which means he or she is energizing the chest voice and creating a very bright, blatant sound. The corresponding physical manifestation of this sound is a high laryngeal placement, pushing the pharynx and thereby tensing all the throat and mouth muscles. So "too open" can establish a negative context.

The word ***passaggio*** means passage: a passage *from* something *to* something. What is the nature of the two "areas" bridged by the vocal *passaggio* and how have we made it so difficult to traverse? To address this subject, we must consider all the elements involved.

In all voices there are two breaks with the *passaggio* lying in the middle. With an experienced voice, the first break is between the chest register and the head-voice area, located at 1st line E-flat. The other break is between the head-voice area and the *falsetto* register, located roughly at C, D, or E-flat above the staff. The *passaggio* is approximately in the middle of the head voice area at the point where dominance shifts from the chest-dominant register to the *falsetto*-dominant register, located at 4th space E-flat—*all in the head voice. It is not the area where the chest voice meets the head voice.*

The following visual hopefully provides a clear picture of registers and *passaggios*. The voice consists of two registers operating in equilibrium, with one register acting as energizer and the other as the synergizer. The chest or synergizer forms the stability for the resonance; the *falsetto* energizer leads the way for pitch and tone color/texture.

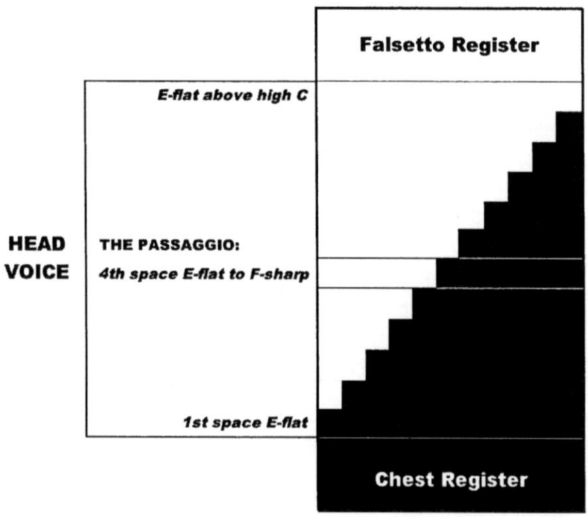

The perfect equilibrium in the head voice is attained through the action of the *falsetto*. For the beauty of the head voice to be available to the singer, *the falsetto must lead the way for the sound*, never the chest. The pure chest register, which one finds at the very bottom of the voice—unless the register has been pushed too high—will break or flow into the head voice at 1st line E-flat. This is true in a child's voice and in any voice that has not been deformed by misuse. If this shift is not allowed but instead the chest register is drawn up as far as it will go, the *falsetto* will not begin to mix in until 2nd space A-flat; the chest texture will continue up to 4th line D. A voice being used this way is commonly referred to as a "Broadway voice" or a "belt voice."

There is also an extension of this technique; a bit more of the *falsetto* is allowed in the voice, but in most instances occurs by covering it, depressing the larynx for more access to the *falsetto*. This voice is often referred to as a "classical belting voice." It actually is the chest voice dominating to the top of the singer's vocal range. Unfortunately for the performer and the audience, this has become the voice of choice in our time. There is no equilibrium, no balance, only stress and pressurization. There is no rich, velvety sound. Only use of the head voice allows equilibrium and balance; only the head voice is stressless with no movement or pressure; only the head voice is natural to singing.

There are several variations of this use of the chest voice, but the figure below represents the "Broadway Belt." When the chest register has been pushed to its maximum in any one area of the voice, an audible break—a crack—will occur, at the point where the voice is trying to make a correction for more *falsetto*. Singers are terrified of a break in the voice, but they should learn from it; they should realize that it is their voice begging for more *falsetto*. This sort of break usually occurs at 2nd line A, 4th space E-flat, or A above the staff, with other possible locations depending on how the voice has been used. Many times these notes will become "holes" in the voice with no phonation at all.

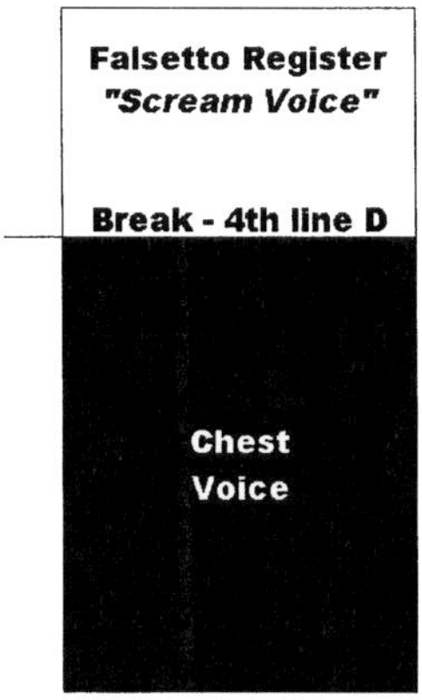

The *passaggio* that most singers talk about is the one located from 4th space E-flat to the F-sharp above. This is the *passaggio* within the head or chest voice, depending on how the singer performs it. This passageway is the balance point between the two registers when they are in equilibrium as illustrated in the first diagram. As long as a singer encourages the proper head voice texture, without forcing the chest register higher than acceptable, the *passaggio* will take care of itself. This texture ensures the proper registration throughout the voice. It does not have to be made to happen; it simply falls where it is as a result of the registration.

If the notes in the *passaggio* present a problem, it is because the registers are out of balance. If one of the registers is not there or is very weak, we must examine the singing voice and find the register within it. If we notice that the *passaggio* is in a different place, the chest voice has probably been pushed too high, setting the *passaggio* at G or A-flat (Giuseppe di Stephano). This situation will throw off every part of the voice. When we sing through the area where the *passaggio* should be, the tone quality is too bright and unstable. That undesirable quality is an audible sign of the inappropriate position of the *passaggio.* Correcting the balance of registers will adjust the *passaggio* in our voice and place it in a position for natural singing. Many other conditions of stress—laryngeal placement and movement and pressure—will fade away.

Let's now return to some observations regarding the term "open." Singing "open" is very confusing to all opera singers and a very difficult road to traverse. Composers of the 17th, 18th, and 19th centuries understood the human voice extremely well. They knew what vowels worked well to produce a beautiful sound or excitement, and they knew what sounds worked best in the *passaggio*, passing into a higher *tessitura.* To sing "open" refers to the absence of constriction in the throat. This freedom allows energy to be employed in order to pass through the *passaggio* effortlessly and without the voice breaking or fluctuating. Many singers today, though, sing "too open," creating all the unwanted constrictions discussed throughout this book. The singer is unable to move to different vowels for fear of having the voice "crack."

The word "*cosi*" at the end of Doretta's aria from Puccini's opera *La Rondine* is a perfect example of a middle voice note needing to spin beautifully to end the aria. One's ability to get enough head voice on the [i] so that the larynx stays free and does not choke off the sound, becomes critical. It becomes clear then that Pavarotti's caveat was actually reference to being "too open." For the rest of us "open" is still a positive term, reflecting freedom in the throat. When the throat is open, it is free; the larynx is not energized through the muscles of the chest register. Being "open" will, as we wish, energize the texture of the head voice sound and allow a beautiful spinning sound to emerge. This is the sound of a major opera singer, not a minor one.

Without being indelicate, this openness of the throat and the wonderful sound produced with this freedom is like one going through puberty. Through this openness, a singer becomes the person that he or she will be for many years.

The F# at the end of the aria "*Liebstod*" on the word "Lust" is another specific example of this freedom in the *passaggio*. Wagner gave his Isolde an (u) vowel, but if one has too much chest in the vocal sound, this F# poses a great deal of difficulty. The vowel needs more head voice than any other vowel may need. But this vowel creates a most beautiful sound. Consider also the line "*mai piu, mai piu . . .*" in Verdi's *Aida*.

Pavarotti has stated often that he learned to sing by using the closed Italian [u] and getting all the other vowels to have the same texture and freedom. When Birgit Nilsson experienced her epiphany one day preparing for a performance in spite of a cold, she stepped into a practice room to warm up but emerged discovering the connection between the head voice and a proper low support. Freedom! She, in her lessons with me, would say that no place should be hard or constricted, but very elastic. And when I speak about the head voice, I think about the *falsetto* singing. Interestingly enough, in Swedish the words "*falsetto*" and "head voice" are the same.

Falsetto singing, according to David Daniels, means easy, beautiful, big, and exciting; it's not what most people think about the *falsetto* sound. We must be careful not to "throw away the baby with the bath water." Think of Jussi Bjoerling at age 14 as a boy alto going through puberty; there was no break or change in his technique—A Full Voiced *Falsetto*—the Head Voice.

Chapter 8
Finding a Voice

Getting Away with Some HEAD VOICE

Ever since I was a child, I wanted to sing; I actually discovered a few years ago that my biological mother was an opera singer of sorts. In grade school and high school, I was always the soloist in the chorus. I had the leads in all the musicals; this was the beginning of my desire to become a singer. Still, I didn't know that it was actually possible to pursue music as a career. As a boy growing up in Iowa, I hadn't ever heard an opera or knew what an aria was; all I knew was musical theater. Finally, in my senior year I heard a concert version of the opera *Faust*. I can remember identifying with the tenor; at the time I was a *tenorino*, very short on range. After this experience, I knew I wanted to be a part of this phenomenon. It was truly bizarre and yet exciting!

I auditioned as a tenor and received a full scholarship to The Catholic University of America in Washington, D.C. I was the classic example of a green but "good" young singer. I didn't know what I was doing to produce a sound that seemed acceptable to others but forged ahead and obtained a degree of success. The natural presence of head voice does give some validity to singing that is in other ways incorrect, and I was lucky enough—or had unconsciously heard and mimicked "real" singers enough who made use of their head voice—to replicate a little bit of the same.

A Little More, But At What Price?

After the first year of study, my voice teacher switched me from tenor to the baritone range; after the second year, he moved me again to bass-baritone. I did roles like Escamillo, Gianni Schicci, and Figaro and I was regional finalist at the Metropolitan Opera Competition as a bass-baritone. (One year later I returned as a tenor.) The jury was freaked. I was getting many solo opportunities in the city, but now F-natural was the top of my voice, and it was not an easy note.

I was learning a technique that did increase the amount of head voice; however, it did so by consciously depressing the larynx. In other words I was getting head voice through the leverage of the chest muscles; I was covering the voice. So, essentially I was singing in my chest voice, but as the second diagram shows, I was pushing the chest register up too high, way past the point which allowed equilibrium. Everything is relative, but I knew my sound was not as free and beautiful as I wanted it to be. I happened to be using enough head voice with little enough constriction; people thought I was pretty good.

Getting Perspective

After completing my undergraduate degree and deciding to continue on for a Masters, I had a cathartic experience. I had been accepted as a bass into the prestigious Montreal International Vocal Competition and I had prepared an opera role, a full recital, and a new piece that all the contestants had to learn. I thought I was ready to sing and win. As I listened to all the other singers, I realized they were singing and physically manipulating the sound in an unnatural way and that I was, also. I didn't like the sound and became so conscious of the muscularity of my voice that I had no desire to continue. I finished the first round and went home.

Taking Charge of Your Own Voice

I stopped singing completely for six months and then I started back slowly; my desire to sing was still strong. This time, however, my criteria for a quality vocal sound had greatly changed. No longer would I allow the manipulations and overt muscularity to be a part of my singing. **The new sound had to be free and easy.** This, of course, sounds rather simplistic, but coming from the amount of physicality I had been applying to my singing, it was difficult to know what "free and easy" really meant. Searching to understand and meet a new standard of quality also led me to a new standard of beauty. **Beautiful**—when was this word ever used in one of my lessons? Never!

(CD Track 5)

In six months I developed—or rather found—a beautiful lyric tenor voice. It was a first rate voice in the rough. I was beginning to understand on my own the concept of the head voice and to develop and apply techniques that helped me achieve a beautiful natural sound, a sound that was free and easy. That year, as a tenor, I entered the Metropolitan Opera Competition and became a Regional Finalist. That year I also was accepted into the apprenticeship program at Wolf Trap in Vienna, Virginia. Also that year I received a contract from Washington Opera for two very nice roles the following season. I was finding considerable success with my newly-found, tenor voice.

(CD Tracks 6, 7)

After completing a very successful summer at Wolf Trap, I moved to New York. This entailed my leaving the position as Head of the Music Department at Trinity College in Washington, D.C., a job that I thought I would have for the rest of my life. The boundaries of my musical career were now set higher, and I realized I could achieve more than I accepted for myself. I was twenty-seven years old and ready to conquer the world. It was 1975.

Halfway There, But Heading In the Wrong Direction

In my first year in New York I was lucky enough to procure artistic management that led to contracts with the Netherlands Opera, Dallas Opera (two roles), and a *La Boheme* with the Goldovsky Opera Company. I felt that I could do anything; however, I still had not totally worked out my "new" voice.

My manager, who didn't think there had been any good music written for the voice after Mozart, encouraged me repeatedly to sing the light Mozart roles. I didn't realize or fully appreciate at the time that Mozart roles would expose the weaknesses in my voice that still needed attention. Filled with so much confidence based upon my limited success thus far, I foolishly caved in and accepted my manager's "wisdom." Rather than trusting my instincts that a little more time perfecting my own voice was in order, I accepted his encouragement to once again go to a voice teacher. I was terrified after what had happened to me earlier, but I thought I would give this New York teacher a chance. This was New York and this teacher was well recognized; what did I have to lose? Based upon hindsight, I lost a great deal.

(CD Track 8)

When I sang with the Dallas Opera, I performed the second tenor role to Jose Carreras and Alfredo Kraus, singers whom I admired and respected and with whom I had many discussions about voice. Carreras invited me to his opening night at the Metropolitan Opera—*Tosca*. He sang beautifully and exemplified the quality voice I was seeking. I also will never forget Krause in the first rehearsal of *I Puritani*, standing there with a cold and yet singing "*A te o cara*" better than I had ever heard it. In fact, I still haven't heard it sung better. Watching and listening to both of these tenors made me realize that my voice still needed to be "retooled" before I could handle the rigors of a leading tenor career.

After the misdirection I'd encountered in voice lessons during college, I swore to myself that I would never step inside another voice teacher's studio. And yet, here I was about the see a teacher recommended by my manager. This teacher told me within the first week that I was going to "thrill the world" with my singing. Within two years I couldn't sing anymore. My voice was heavy, dark, and totally inefficient; however, promises that my voice was right around the next corner were plentiful. This teacher was very charismatic and for me the charisma lasted four years.

(CD Track 9)

During that time my voice did change, but now it was bright and edgy. Gone was the richness and warmth I was rediscovering after my first misdirection. The voice was still "good enough," acceptable within the realm of today's singers, but it wasn't what I expected of it. I was singing on the regional circuit throughout the U.S., but more and more my voice just was not holding up. I'd get laryngitis or often had to sing with a bad throat. The rigors of the final week of rehearsal with all the singing would tire my voice. It was not a pleasant time. Once home from each of these engagements, I would listen to a recording of the performances, if available; I hated what I heard in my voice. All the beauty was gone; my musicality would get me through, but the sheer sound of what had been a beautiful voice was no longer there. I finally left this second voice teacher, went back to work on my own, and moved to Columbia Artists Management.

Back in the Driver's Seat, Heading Home

Once again I stopped singing and stopped studying. Fortunately, when I first moved to New York I established a voice studio. By this time I had a full studio with an assistant who taught when I was out of town performing. I reduced the amount of performing and used this time to reestablish the "beautiful" voice toward which I had been heading. My studio gave me the opportunity to work on my own voice as well as direct my students in a way that they could perfect their voices. But I hadn't yet connected the goal I sought with singing in the head voice; I called it "free and easy."

In 1987, after two years of teaching and reworking my own voice, I was singing Walther in *Die Meistersinger von Nürnberg* for four months in England. I heard from Michael Cordovana, my friend back in Washington, that he was organizing a Master Class with Birgit Nilsson. He asked me if I wanted to sing for her. Although I knew nothing of opera in Iowa, I learned quickly who Birgit Nilsson was and fell in love with her voice; she had been an idol of mine since beginning my career. In high school I saw Birgit Nilsson on *The Ed Sullivan Show* singing "*In questa reggia*" from *Turandot*. Of course, I wanted to sing for her! I considered what role I'd sing. I had been asked many times to sing certain Wagnerian roles and always declined; I was too young and felt my voice would never fit the character. But after *Die Meistersinger von Nürnberg*, I felt ready; I was no longer singing the "old" way, so I decided that I would prepare the role of Sigmund to sing for her.

I was fortunate to work with Ms. Nilsson privately one hour a day for three days. In Washington, DC, few singers have an opportunity to work privately with someone of her caliber. I was ecstatic when on the third day she invited me to Germany to work with her for a month. We worked at least four and five hours a day, often more, seven days a week on vocalizing and repertoire. It was truly one of the great experiences of my life. Many times she would sing along or take the part of Sieglinda. It was a thrill.

One of the first things Birgit said to me in the Master Class was, "My dear, use at least some head voice if you have any." Before the end of the month in Germany, I realized what she meant. Each time I previously reworked my voice, I had tried to return to the standard of "**easy and beautiful**." What I had never done, though, was make the connection between that goal and the **head voice**. Working with Birgit Nilsson showed me the connection; it was incredibly powerful. She wanted me to sing that way and I could do that. I was singing in my head voice, and she was corroborating its existence in my sound.

The head voice wasn't just for the lighter roles. She even expected Wagner to be sung in the head voice. Many times she would produce one of her high C's or B's and the sheer intensity was exhilarating. Head voice is not just in the realm of the Kathleen Battle's of singing. Even I could sing this way; every singer can sing in the head voice and improve the quality of sound, sound that is "beautiful," "free," "easy," "efficient," "stressless," and big.

Birgit and I became very good friends and remained so until her death. She was a remarkable woman with a remarkable intellect. She too faced misdirection in her vocal training, and she too had to figure it out on her own. She found the "secret" to quality sound, though, better and faster than most.

After that month in Germany, my life changed and so did my teaching. Teaching was now the area of singing that excited me the most, and I shifted my primary focus to teaching from that time on. My singing had never been better, but performance had taken its toll on me. My voice was still evolving into the potential I knew I had, although I maintained a rigorous performance schedule.

(CD Track 16)

I took on a limited number of roles when I returned to New York: Pollione in *Norma* with the Minnesota Opera, Cavaradossi with Atlanta Opera, and a series of Don Jose's in London, Tokyo, Melbourne, and Sydney. All the while I was working on adjusting my technique to add more head voice. I sang for Birgit when she came to New York, and I sent her tapes of my performances which she would critique. These were the best voice lessons I had ever had.

(CD Tracks 11, 12, 15)

Many performances are especially memorable, particularly the *Die Meistersinger von Nürnberg* in England with Opera North, the first new production of this opera in England in twenty years. I sang seventeen performances of Walther, one every three days with a great chorus and orchestra, conducted by David Lloyd Jones from the heart. I also sang a production of *La Fanciulla del West* with Virginia Opera. Minnie in that production was soprano June Fisk. What a sound she made; it was like singing with Renata Tebaldi. *Carmen* in Sydney with Maria Ewing was another memorable experience; she is a great artist with a truly fantastic voice. One of the newspaper reviews read "Striny and Ewing had a capacity audience of 15,000 captivated . . . they provided a thrilling and unforgettable night."

(CD Track 13)

Birgit also arranged a private audition at Bayreuth with Wolfgang Wagner for me. This opportunity and the experience of singing Sigmund on stage with the set of *Siegfried* and with Wagner as my only audience was extremely thrilling.

I wrote this book because I am very fortunate to have experienced the opportunities I've had in spite of the human obstacles and errors I've faced. My regret is that I trusted voice teachers blindly; I didn't have the courage to discuss my reservations and to challenge what they were asking me to do. I regret that I didn't trust my instincts which were guiding me in a direction toward singing with the head voice. Perhaps my understanding of head voice is clearer and has better depth because I have had the advantage of comparison. Most probably I would not have had the time, because of performances, to reach this understanding and to write it down. I hope that some of what I have learned will help others follow their desires to sing without derailment.

The title of this book, *Head First: The Language of the Head Voice*, refers to the two ways a singer must be trained or the two ways a singer must train him or herself. *Use your head and use your head voice.*

Chapter 9
About Teachers

"A soprano is about B flats, high C's, and higher notes, and not about out-shouting an orchestra in the chest voice."

- Birgit Nilsson

"Opera is about singing—except that great singing was part of a Golden Age that has disappeared forever." This is a quotation from Patrick J. Smith, past editor of *Opera News*.

What happened? Was it the water; the ozone layer; Mt. St. Helen's? How is it that we read a comment like this and agree thinking: "Of course, the Golden Age is gone forever." To understand what has happened, I think we really need to divide the category **Opera** into two parts—Opera Theater and Opera. Understandably, most of what we hear today is Opera Theater. Fast becoming the norm in opera production, Opera Theater consists of a crossover vocal sound and beautiful people overacting. The natural step in Opera Theater is to bring on the microphones and the synthesizers, which are already being discussed in *Opera News*. But once again, what happened? Real opera consists of voices of the Golden Age based on a quality of sound almost gone from the stage. It is a sound based upon the head voice, the rich velvety sound from a time past. It is a sound still heard but growing faint—Karita Matilla, Ruth Ann Swenson, Lauren Flanigan, Renee Fleming.

The Lost Art?

A few years ago at the Met, I heard Monserrat Caballe sing the role of Elisabetta in *Don Carlo*. In the Garden scene of Act II, there are two pianissimo high A naturals that the soprano faces. The first Caballe sang softly, but it had a tiny glitch; it stopped for an instant. As the second high A approached, I thought she'd sing the note a little louder to make sure it didn't break. No, she surprised us; she sang the second A even softer than the first. How exquisite, how amazingly she spun the tone through the theater! This is great singing. Not only did she have the ability to sing a pianissimo A natural, but it was also incredibly beautiful.

Such wonderful singers like Caballe, Tucker, Nilsson, Bjoerling, Pavarotti, Price, and Sutherland are hallmarks in the phenomenon of voice. The way they sing is a gift that has allowed them to maintain and nurture their beautiful sound. *But it is also a technique.* This technique can be awakened in all of us because it lies very close to the surface. It is a natural way of singing, but it is vulnerable to disruption from constriction that can either blemish the natural voice or derail it completely.

The Wrong Knowledge

The aesthetics of singing has been lost. The thrill of a "golden" sound that fills a 4,000 seat theater—a sound that is so beautiful and so free that we cannot imagine it coming from a human being—is no longer a part of our experience. What I call *classical belting* has become the standard: loud throaty voices barking out text at an audience. No longer is the inherent beauty of the voice a consideration. Why not? The real problem is not that the singing quality has declined, although it has. The quality of vocal instruction has changed. Proper technique and developing the aesthetics of singing are not taught any more. It is no longer taught because it is rarely heard any more. Fewer and fewer singers in the profession of operatic performance are engaging in this quality of sound, this texture of the voice called the **head voice**. The next generation of performers hasn't the models to emulate except through recordings of by-gone singers.

This subject is very difficult to discuss because one person's trash is another person's treasure, and this subject involves more subjective analysis than most. Return to chapter one; it begins with developing good listening from the best performers of the "lost art." Let none sway the reader from this point. This problem, this condition in the vocal world is very real. I am more convinced than ever that we have reached a point of pandemic in the world of pure operatic vocal production. Dinosaurs did not just disappear, consumed into animal heaven in the blink of an eye. There was a cause and effect to their extinction that science has for ages been determining. As painful as this subject is for both singers and teachers, it must be addressed, or the voice of the "Golden Age" will permanently fade into oblivion like the dinosaur. Today many operas in the repertory are being shelved because producers can no longer cast singers who can satisfy even the basic needs of the work. There are no singers to fill these challenging and demanding roles anymore—*Turandot, Aida, Der Ring des Nibelungen, I Puritani. . . .*

On a Saturday opera broadcast, a panel of experts all agreed that there are no longer any baritones of the caliber of Merrill and Warren. In the March (1999) issue of *Opera News*, Albert Innaurato bemoaned the loss of mezzos who had true Verdian voices. We all know that sopranos of the caliber of Price, Nilsson, and Sutherland no longer exist; the beautiful voices of Bjoerling, Corelli, Vickers, and Tucker also have been silenced.

Most of these great singers amazingly just walked out of some obscure part of the world, not even knowing how to read music, and walked onto the great stages of the world. Singing on a high level requires the nurturing of a seed of sound which is free and beautiful, not the overt manipulation of muscles. This seed is found in all of us and was encouraged through street music and folk music in Spain and Italy. "*O sole mio*" is a classic example of this point. This selection may have been sung so much that it hyperbolizes in a comical or negative way the Italian culture, but it reflects the quintessential qualities of beautiful natural singing with its standard of sound. Parents would sing and the children would copy the sounds, sounds that were singer's sounds.

We must listen to that sound; not feel the muscles. *Beautiful and easy* must once again become the criteria for singing in the voice studio and on the stage. We need voice cultivation, not voice production and that doesn't happen without a re-education of our teachers. The art of singing is one of the highest art forms in our human experience; it must be preserved. It isn't to be handled like weightlifting.

Leontyne Price's statement about the love she has for her voice says it all. It is not that Leontyne Price is different from the rest of us. It's just that she uses a different way of singing than we do and she has the insight to understand its importance and the commitment to preserve it. She is obviously looking for beauty, not loudness. She loves her voice not only because it sounds and is beautiful but also because producing it feels right. She makes sounds that enable her to fully encompass the experience of the music she creates. The music was written for voices like hers, voices that could spin out top notes, sing pianissimo high notes, and have such an inherent beauty that it would bring the listeners to tears—**simply because of the sound.**

Verdi, Strauss, and Donizetti wrote for this type of voice, and Wagner wanted his operas sung in an Italianate fashion. These composers knew the voice, wrote for it, and wanted the performers to produce that lush sound, a sound based upon the head voice. We can return to that beautiful sound, but we must teach the singers of the next generation the quality of the head voice, and nurture them as they develop this sound with this technique—unconstricted, free, and beautiful.

Call a Spade a Spade

So what exactly are we talking about here? I've mentioned generically the failure of vocal instruction. But what is the solution to a performance art that is spiraling downward? We are talking about the **Head Voice**. Singers today are no longer using their head voices, and teachers are no longer teaching its use.

What is the **Head Voice**? If we look at the April 13, 1996 issue of *Opera News* we see the following phrases and words describing various voices:

Column A	Column B
silvery, youthful	*those pianissimos frightened me*
intrinsically musical	*lacks the ease*
limpid and luminous	*less refined in texture*
youthful beauty of tone	*not enough vocal heft and color*
ripe enveloping tone	*squally tone*
no constraint in tonal emission	*unrestrained vibrato*
warm and golden	*grainy*
expressive vocal colors	*chirped prettily*
luscious baritone	*registers need better connection*
caressing sweetness of tone	*steely top*
voluptuous, caressing quality	*bright*
deep soft roundness	

These words are not just describing the texture or sound of a voice, but really are describing a **way of singing**. Let's not overlook cause and effect. The voice can be produced in two distinctly different ways, bringing about two distinctly different textures. Column A describes voices that are **head voice dominant**. These are voices produced by a set of muscles that do not move the larynx in order to change pitch and vowel. These are *falsetto*-oriented voices. Column B describes voices that are **chest voice dominant**. These are voices that must move the larynx for changes of pitch and vowel. One texture is unconstricted and free; the other is not. One has a beautiful, effortless sound; the other is brittle and sounds like it is belted.

How It Works

What does the larynx have to do with singing, and who cares whether it moves? The larynx houses the vocal apparatus. Because of its proximity to the generated vocal sound and as long as it is left open (relaxed), the larynx acts as the prime resonator for the voice. When the larynx moves, the vocal apparatus constricts. It tightens up and closes by degrees with the amount of movement involved. This movement is brought on by singing with the extrinsic laryngeal muscles, used by most people for speech and shouting. These muscles are referred to in singing as **chest muscles** because the frequencies that are produced by this texture of sound are low and are felt through vibration in the large bones of the body closest to the generator, the chest. For hundreds of years, the sound was actually thought to have been produced in the chest.

The muscles of the **head voice** are found within the larynx, and they do not move the larynx with changes of vowel and pitch. This non-movement allows the larynx to be an incredibly efficient resonator for the sound; its positioning is now relaxed and stable, not constantly in motion. Strike a tuning fork and it produces such a resonant pitch. Barely touch the prongs and the effort to maintain the pitch is increased. Grab the prongs and the sound stops altogether. There are in nature many other metaphors to show the difference between constricted and unconstricted sound.

The **head voice** produces frequencies that are around 3000 cps (cycles per second). These frequencies set in sympathetic vibration the small bones and cartilage closest to the generated sound which are found in the head. Movement of the larynx creates constriction, and vibration loss reduces effectiveness in producing the quality and texture of sound that represents the "lost art."

The lovely *pianissimos* of Price, Caballe, and Milanov have easily filled the largest opera houses with "limpid, luminous, warm, golden, luscious, caressing, round tones." The fortes were equally beautiful and impressive. What about the *pianissimos* of the **chest voice**? There is no such thing. The chest voice needs the forced drive of a lot of breath pressure. This pressure must be maintained continuously or the voice will break. This pressure is needed because the texture of the chest voice is produced with the larynx in such constriction and closure that the breath must be forced, not fed, through the larynx to produce the sound. It is very much like a garden hose with a kink in it. In this state, backing off to *pianissimo* is next to impossible for those with chest dominant voice. It becomes difficult and frightening for those with just a little chest rolling around.

In chest-dominant voices, as the performer sings higher, the larynx moves up and closes even more. The singer tries to accommodate this movement by opening the mouth wide, hoping to give the larynx the room it needs. The breath pressure increases to maximum because the larynx is so closed. The tone grows more "squally, grainy, steely, and bright," and the "lack of ease" causes such overt muscularity that the vibrato becomes "unrestrained." The voice is now "*intrinsically [un]musical*" with a closed respiratory system.

Great Singers as Teachers

Last year at one of New York's most prestigious conservatories, Leontyne Price gave a Master Class. The best students from each of the teachers at the school participated. Price was at somewhat of a loss because none of these students could sing the way she does. She didn't mean sing as *well* as she does; she meant they didn't sing *with a similar technique*. Everything that went into making her one of the greatest sopranos of our time was lost on these students. During the five days of the Master Class, they had no idea how she produced those exquisite sounds or how she created the phrases that she was demonstrating to them. The phrases she demonstrated took on the musicality of her basic sound, of her gorgeous sound! She could only apply band-aids to a problem that was too deep to resolve. What a shame. Today's singers have no understanding of the sound and techniques of a true master. These students, unfortunately, chalked their inadequacy up to the idea that she was, of course, "Leontyne Price." The students failed to understand and learn the magic she was giving to them, and ironically they will be the dinosaurs who fail to learn and adapt. They certainly did not appreciate that she was showing them a different way to sing.

What does this incident say about the instructors of these "gifted" students? Those voice teachers nodded their heads as if Leontyne Price's approach was just what they espoused in their studios, though it certainly was not. If their techniques were correct, wouldn't their students have produced the sound and texture before the Master Class? They didn't; they couldn't. They and their teachers hadn't understood the difference. They hadn't understood the point of singing with the **head voice**, using **head voice** vowels and texture that would both keep the respiratory system relaxed and feed unforced breath through the sound.

Leontyne Price's singing is all head voice right down to the dusky toned bottom of her voice. The students' voices were all in their throat: constricted, edgy, shallow sounds with shrill high notes. To be a truly great singer, one must first sing in a way that great singers sing. For performers like Price and others, that ability involves the use of the head voice and the technique that produces an exquisite, lush, velvety sound that with little effort can fill the largest opera houses of the world.

Today's teachers do not hear the element in the voice that contains its beauty. We still have our natural singers, but with each decade they are fewer and fewer. Not even Italy is producing natural voices. The reason, without any doubt in my mind, is the prominence of popular music. Children are singing along with the radio and using the sounds in the full voice and the *falsetto* that are used in rock and pop. These are chest-dominant sounds that eventually will weaken the head voice. This weakening diminishes the possibility of open unconstricted singing, the kind of singing that creates beautiful sound.

Muscles! Muscles! Muscles!

Teaching voice became more tangible with the discovery of the laryngoscope around the turn of the 20th century. Voice researchers looked down the throat of a singer and saw those two tiny bands vibrating. Singers and teachers now felt that because those bands were vibrating in the throat that was where the sound should be felt. This concept was the beginning of the end for vocal pedagogy; it misdirected where our focus should be in vocal instruction. Along with this tangible discovery about the vocal chords, singers and teachers felt that because one could see the mechanism, it, therefore, was important to know what its component parts were called and what their functions were.

The terminology was no longer just "head," "chest," and "*falsetto*," but now a myriad of muscles which entered into the explanation of the singing process and, of course, had to be understood. It was up to the teacher to know just what all these muscles did. The new terminology now became "laryngeal pharynx," "thyrohyoids," "stylopharyngeal," "sternothyroids," and "cricopharyngeals." What a mess! Many teachers no longer focused or listened to a beautiful sound. They were concerned with manipulating the arytenoids, or at least think they were. This misperception and misdirection continues today in voice studios. Teachers knowingly or subconsciously justify themselves as voice teachers because they now know more terminology than any voice student would want to know. They claim that with this knowledge they now could "*build a voice*." If we strengthen this muscle and pull that cartilage; brace this and support that; lift this, etc., we will then have a quality voice. This situation is like a physical therapist who thinks a ballet dancer can be created merely by manipulating the muscles of the legs.

Armed with anatomy books, legions of voice teachers have marched into their voice lessons ready to slay the ugly-toned dragon with the pull of the arytenoid or the tug of the cricoid. Many in this band of teachers have never sung professionally; therefore, have developed only the limited skill of a dilettante, if that. Their medical-sounding knowledge impresses hundreds of students who are eager to put their faith in someone who promises to help them achieve their dreams and make them a vocal wonder. But if we want to learn how to play tennis, do we go to a teacher who has never played the game, who only knows the names of the muscles in the arms or the legs? Definitely not! If we want to learn to sing, should we go to someone who only plays the piano? Absolutely not!

What has happened to the role of the voice teacher? Those who have ever sung in the shower may have felt as if they understood the voice as well as anyone. And if they also played the piano they could qualify as a voice teacher. These "teachers" may feel fully confident that they can make a difference, that they understand how Bjoerling, Milanov, Ponselle, and the other greats sang. These "teachers" believe they sing in essentially the same way themselves. These "teachers" believe the difference between the greats and themselves is that God gave the great singers better voices. WRONG! Singing in a particular way produces a particular sound, good or bad.

These same "teachers" believe that if our sound is not "in the ballpark" with the great singers, that their students are not doing what they asked for. Or they claim God just didn't give this individual the same talent. These "teachers" attempt to make their students sing "in the image and likeness" of great singers, failing to understand that the student's discovery of proper technique and the exquisite sound is the real goal in vocal instruction. In learning the right sound a proper technique will come forth. The sound will be a natural sound; it will have the lush, velvety quality of the great singers.

Luisa Tetrazzini comments in her book *The Art of Singing*: "The country is overrun with inferior teachers in singing; men and women who have failed to get before the public, turn to teaching without any practical experience, ruining many good voices." Unfortunately, time has not made Tetrazzini's remarks obsolete. The poor student is at the mercy of someone who does not know how to sing but only knows the physiognomy of the human body. If this philosophy of vocal instruction permeates the rest of society, we will certainly find ourselves in a sorry state of affairs. Voice teachers must do more to understand good sound and how it is created. Voice teachers must change their pedagogy. We must learn from the "masters of the voice" before they are all gone. We must preserve the wealth of good singing that is only to be found through the **Head Voice**.

What is the sound of the styloglossus muscle anyway? That's impossible to tell. But one can know the sound of the head voice and the chest voice. Ask any great singer if he or she wants to know the different muscles involved in singing. Ask yourself if you think that knowing the names of the muscles used in walking will make walking easier. In walking, we actually do know what the various muscles do, but in singing, we do not. If we're singing properly we're unaware of any sensations. Great singers often exclaim that their singing voice is outside of their bodies because they are unaware of any sensation. Average people make a similar observation about sensing how they walk. What overt muscular sensations do we get from walking? None. The mechanism is in preserving equilibrium. We sense balance; we walk from here to there—that's all.

In addition to the failure to understand good vocal technique, voice teachers are teaching breathing as if preparing students for a weightlifting competition. Incorrectly, it involves the degree of laryngeal stability used in moving pianos. As the great teacher Lamperti said, "There is nothing so meaning-less as a mechanically controlled tone. It lacks beauty." Once again, the word beauty is being associated with freedom from "mechanical control," freedom from setting the breath as if we were about to move a piano.

Tetrazzini further comments that: "Much has been said about the Italian Method of Singing. It is a question of whether anyone really knows what the phrase means. If there is a right way to sing, then all other ways must be wrong." THIS IS ABSOLUTELY TRUE! She further states: "The height of vocal art is to have no apparent method but to be able to sing with perfect facility from one end of the voice to the other, emitting all notes clearly and yet with power and with each note sounding the same in quality and tonal beauty as the one before or after." So a singer should want his or her voice to be at the disposal of reflex, the guardian of natural movement: no overt muscular manipulations, no strenuous support or anchoring; just singing and feeling the breath through the sound.

Limited Knowledge, Good Intentions Limited

There is another type of pedagogy that is quite common in teaching voice. It is based on "just singing." Take what you have as a voice; modify some of the vowels; learn where to breathe in a piece of music; learn and polish the languages, and there you have it! For good young singers, this can actually be the safest way to proceed. Intuition will help resolve technical problems because no one interferes with a singer's basic instinct of sound. However, if one has problems with the voice, this type of teaching does not help a fledgling vocal performer to correct the problem. These singers are likely to find themselves in trouble one day and will need a deeper understanding of what they had been doing right in order to return to their "natural" voice.

Most voice teachers were never able to pursue a singing career of their own; they just didn't sing well enough. In any other field this would have disqualified them from employment. In voice, this consideration does not even enter the picture. Anyone can hang out a shingle declaring to be a *bona fide*, certified voice teacher. These people too often are given *carte blanche* by us. Insecure singers will study with these teachers and become frustrated with their own voice. They will start to teach and perpetuate this negative cycle of pedagogy.

Formal education plays a big part in furthering this misleading cycle. We all think that we have to go to college or a conservatory to succeed in the music profession. We, therefore, put ourselves at the mercy of an administration that very rarely is qualified to make a "voice teacher" decision for a student. Consider also the myriad of courses used as filler but called requirements. For a performance degree, courses in history and composition are not or intrinsically necessary for a performance career. And so for four years or more, we may easily be chained to a teacher and a curriculum that doesn't work for everyone the same way. We may not know that we are stuck, but we are. And this circumstance happens at a time in our lives when a good vocal foundation should be well established.

After the college experience, we naturally think we are ready to greet the world of vocal performance. But really we are well on our way to a life fraught with the anxiety and frustration of still needing to learn how to sing. We will have invested at least four to six years in improper instruction at a college or university and paid an incredible amount of money as well; an investment in vocal preparation essentially dumped down the drain.

We now continue vocal study outside the college setting in the real world. We work a full time job to pay for basic necessities of food and shelter, at the same time attempting to establish a vocal career seeking further instruction via private lessons. We aren't ready for the performance world, but we have no idea where to go to resolve our vocal problems. Meanwhile our friends are either continuing their further education in a medical school or a law school, or playing in orchestras, or getting married and starting a family. We are the performers who have temporary jobs working with computers while our parents wonder why we continue this plight and why we don't just settle down and develop a real career.

Many singers have experienced a glimpse of the wonderful phenomenon of beautiful singing that has been locked up inside of them. Only a few have more than a glimpse of the "lost art." These singers know that the art of singing does exist and that the quest is worth pursuing. They know what it is like to tap into the power and pleasure of the voice. They are caught in a physical and psychological web of being a singer but not being able to perform as an artist—if at all!

Instrumentalists can walk away from their instruments, put them in the closet, and never look at them again. It may be difficult to put the passion behind them, but it can be done. For singers it is impossible. Singers must deal with the fact and the existence of their voice every day because it is their body. Singing is inherent to character and cannot be so easily separated. The physical component of the body/voice combined with the psychological component of being a creative artist creates a very potent world of frustration.

Enjoy Making Music

So, how important is having a good teacher from the start of one's vocal training? It is extremely important! Unfortunately, the chances of finding a good teacher who understands vocal sound and technique are very slim in today's market. The student must take the initiative and must carefully maneuver to avoid the pitfalls and quagmires of improper instruction and misleading teachers. He or she must use common sense and must use the great voices of the past as a guide.

The best teacher for singing at this stage might be someone who allows and guides a student to experiment with his or her voice without causing damage created by heavy repertoire. The student needs someone who will not push for a particular sound, but will allow the student to discover his or her own sound. This means the student must take the responsibility for his or her own voice and this requires drive and maturity. Many students just out of college aren't trained to search for the right voice teacher or to think independently.

Some of the responsibility morally does fall upon the voice teacher. A teacher must be supportive and encourage a student to take responsibility for change. The decision concerning the right method and the right teacher should be mutually arrived at, but ultimately, the student cannot turn over the responsibility for his or her voice to anyone else. It wasn't egotism that led Leontyne

Price to declare she loved her own voice. She was simply toasting "the gift," because to her, it certainly felt like it.

Another common "voice teacherism" involves physical manipulation of the larynx. This is pretty frightening. How a teacher can actually believe that he or she knows where the larynx should be, or how it should feel, or how far away it should be from the hyoid bone is patently absurd and many times harmful. Many teachers will physically manipulate the larynx while a student is singing. "Get your hands off my throat!" should be the only response to that type of situation.

Physical manipulation is often seen as a viable component of vocal instruction, as easy to reach as breathing. But when we consider the thirty-one muscles that connect at the hyoid bone along with all the cartilage, common sense should tell a student and his or her teacher that physical manipulation is no better than trying to win the lottery. Isn't a student's throat relaxed when he or she is not making sound? This is how the throat should be when a student sings properly: Jaw relaxed, so as to almost start to drool, soft palate released and just hanging there, breath feeding the sound without tension.

Determine the elements of the process that create vocal tension; and eliminate them from the vocal production. A student may have to diminish the sound to a *pianissimo* initially to find this freedom, but he or she will at least have a seed to nurture. Listen to the sounds associated with the release of tension in the larynx and use those sounds as a compass to free the mechanism. There are many options but the sense of feeling is best, especially when learning effortless singing like the great singers. Tension begets tension but an unconstricted larynx sets the stage for the golden sound of a great singer. Find a track that does not involve tension. Use a set of vowels that do not constrict the throat. Use a dynamic that will allow freedom. Driving and pushing a sound is not freedom, but is merely reveling in one's own ego, or the ego of the teacher. Loud, throaty high notes seem to be the menu of the day in vocal performance. No one can object to loud, but no audience wants loud and ugly. Loud and beautiful is one of the glories of singing. They are only produced with the **head voice**.

Tension can be felt, but the element that results in great singing is not felt except in a secondary manner through resonance. Even then, many great singers speak of their voices as being "outside themselves," "out of their body," "out front." So, in order that the rest of us have the sensations the great singers speak of, we must be using our voices in the same way they use their voices. For those singers who don't yet have the sensations, though, they must be led into an experience of singing that had been previously overlooked. The student must be led by a competent voice teacher away from the seductive use of physical space and overt muscularity in order to create a different sound.

The Best There Is

I was fortunate to have worked with Birgit Nilsson, an exception to the rule that it is difficult to study with a great singer because he or she just wants the student to imitate his or her sound. Birgit only wanted me to imitate the way she sang, not to imitate her sound. Once I was singing in the head voice, the sound I produced was my own, not Birgit Nilsson's. Because Birgit had worked on her own voice throughout her career, unassisted by a voice teacher, she understood what great singing really entails. When singing is at a very high level, there is no overt sense of the mechanism, only the product of that mechanism.

How then would a great singer know what to tell a student who is not yet at that level? "Feel nothing" does not really help unless a student is guided to the proper way to produce that unique sound. Great singers usually don't talk about the larynx or the throat. They only speak of the breath; that is all they feel. Birgit would say, "The energy starts down here (pointing to the lower abdomen) then it somehow connects with the sound in the mask; there is nothing in between. Your sound resonates in your head like the sound board of a violin."

(CD Track 13)

When many great singers turn to teaching, they will have developed so many bad habits over the span of their career that the quality of their sound may be gone and the integrity of their instruction may be questionable. These bad habits always involve a sense of muscularity that, unfortunately, can be passed along to students. And so, non-performing voice teachers, as well as great singers who turn to teaching, need to be viewed carefully. Birgit Nilsson never approached me as anything but a consummate performer and a gifted teacher. Fortunately, when she decided to retire, Birgit's voice was still in wonderful shape . . . and it remained that way until her death. . . . She understood what was needed to help produce an operatic voice. She always had a sense of her own **head voice**, which was what she wanted me to use in my singing. I wasn't supposed to sound like Birgit Nilsson; I was to emulate a way of singing. That's what a voice lesson should embody.

Your Job as a Student

In his *Practical Reflections on Figured Singing*, Giovanni Mancini wrote: "Art consists of knowing where nature directs us, and to what we have been destined: understanding at once the gifts of nature and cultivating them easily. Man can perfect himself; how sure is the harvest for the attentive farmer, who has observed and understood the different seeds which are fecund in diverse types of earth." Great singers like Nilsson, Price, Sutherland, Pavarotti, and Merrill have innately understood the nature of the voice and like Mancini's farmer have pursued the cultivation of their own "seed."

The noted teacher and author Cornelius Reid writes in his *Dictionary of Vocal Terminology* that "Procedures for cultivating the voice center on the development and integration of the two vocal registers which were termed the *voce di petto*, or chest voice and the *falsetto*." Unfortunately, methods using this approach take the meaning of Mancini's "seed" to be *two separated parts needing to be strengthened and joined.* This suggests alteration of the seed, not cultivation of a natural singing sound.

A seed is an organic whole, itself containing the essence which one desires to grow. So within the seed of sound is the kernel of the full sound. The seed is already complete; it only needs cultivation, not genetic alteration.

Most teachers look at the "seed" and say, "Ah, but there are no roots." They decide to paste on some roots. They then see it will need leaves; so they paste them on also. This development creates a voice that becomes not real and authentic, not natural, but something made up, a concoction of bits and pieces from sources other than what the student can create. The seed needs to be planted and nurtured and nourished. Only then will it produce the real product, an authentic, natural sound found among the great singers of today and the great singers of the Golden Age of Vocal Music.

To find the seed, a singer must take a middle voice sound and reduce it to its lowest dynamic where both registers will function in an efficient, balanced manner. The mouth and jaw will be perfectly relaxed, and the two registers, with the *falsetto* mechanism in primary control of the sound, will be coordinated. The singer with this environment just needs to think "beautiful sound." The chest register will respond to the degree of *falsetto* contained within the sound. The sound will now be whole, complete, and full, lacking only the nurturing to work within a large pitch and dynamic range.

With a chest-dominant pedagogy, voices produce throaty, edgy, metallic, thin, shrill, and ugly sounds. The purity of sound hardly exists any longer because it had never really been understood by the singer or the voice teacher.

We occasionally witness young prodigies who sing with a natural sound. To maintain it and nurture it through schools, conservatories, wrong teachers and coaches is almost an impossible task. Our teachers are dictating muscular actions, trying to strengthen muscles. They hope and plan for the "total product" to come together at the conclusion of the process. But it never does. We may even presume that many teachers and coaches feel puzzled or frustrated by the "less-than-sublime" results they are receiving in their studios. What is to be expected by supporting an incorrect and constricted technique? In her *New York Times* article (11/13/05) "The End of the Great Big American Voice," Anne Midgette posed a number of questions concerning this loss in the world of opera. By article's end, it was clear that no one knew the answers to these questions.

Ego and the need to control will many times reign supreme in the vocal studio, especially when there is a piece missing in the teacher's knowledge: "I only teach women—I only teach men—there is no need to ever use the *falsetto*—over 'high C' just spread and brighten—there are 5 registers—there is no such thing as registers—there should not be a '*passaggio*'—that's your whistle register . . ." These red-light statements are cover-ups, and the truly correct answer should just be "I don't understand it either." It is very difficult for the young singer, who is off the track, to sort out the information and find his or her way back. They lack trust in the teaching profession and rightly so. To these singers I repeat, "**Use your head first.**"

Chapter 10
Getting In the Zone

Letting It Happen

If students are no longer implicitly willing to place confidence and faith in a voice teacher, but also are unable to understand and appreciate the idea of singing in the **head voice**—the idea of "feeling nothing"—how can they begin to approach this different way of thinking and reacting? They must trust their body's reflexive self, the self that is awakened with proper use of energy. This is the self that circumvents the conscious attempts at manipulation.

If we've been trained and encouraged to trust the reflexive self, nervousness will cease, and enjoyment of both singing and developing a role will be the outcome of our process. This is when a singer "zones in." This is when the sound becomes one with the audience, creating an atmosphere in an auditorium which is electrifying. W. Timothy Gallwey reinforces the description of this special moment in his book *The Inner Game of Tennis* when he writes "If there is any theme that dominates the reports of 'zone experience,' it is this subtle freedom from intervention, from volition and thought, and finally from consciousness itself."

A voice that is controlled by the part of the brain that initiates reflex is singing without interference of the conscious mind. This state of mind and body is referred to by many athletes as being "in the zone." But with experience both in the studio and on the stage, that performer must be able to relinquish conscious effort and control of the vocal mechanism and allow the body to perform on the basis of preparation, artistic instinct and talent, and physical reflexes. It is psychologically uplifting when a performer knows he or she is "in the zone." Everything works harmoniously and the quality of vocal production is perfect. Voice students and professional singers reach their potential as singers when this surrender of conscious attention to technique becomes their way of singing and thinking. Gallwey further observes that, "It is the constant 'thinking' activity, the ego-mind, which interferes with the natural process." D. T. Suzuki mirrors the concept of an unconscious reflex in the forward to *Zen in the Art of Archery* (Eugen Herrigel, author). There he comments that, ". . . as soon as we reflect, deliberate, and conceptualize, the original unconsciousness is lost and a thought interferes. . . . The arrow is off the string but does not fly straight to the target, nor does the target stand where it is. Calculation, which is miscalculation, sets in. Man is a thinking reed but his great works are done when he is not calculating and thinking 'childlikeness' must be restored with long years of training in self-forgetfulness." As singers, we never will reach our best until we can surrender the conscious techniques and just sing.

When we are in this "frame of mind," music is made. But we don't make it. Sounds get sung, but we do not manufacture them. It is an "out of this world" experience that parallels the "out of body" "feel nothing" experience that the great singers refer to. This is why many great singers refer to their voice as a "gift." They don't know why they have this gift, but they are thankful that it is theirs, theirs to share. If this reflex is blocked the unconstricted singing process stops; the magic is gone, and the body reverts to overt muscular manipulation in an attempt to continue. The voice no longer feels like a gift because the singer must resort to overt physical manipulation. The singer cannot recover the "zone" and must ply the old ways, the ones proven to be an inefficient means to their potential.

Singing with the **head voice** fosters this "in the zone" philosophy. The performer is "in the zone" when the mind is "at the moment"—not before it, not after it. How can those of us who are merely decent singers reach such a state? The answer is that we must sing in a manner that relies upon reflex. Then our voices will be free, unconstricted. Then we will be able to produce the rich velvety texture of a free, natural singing voice. When we sing in our **head voice**, there is no overt manipulation of muscles, regardless of the dynamic asked for in the music, or regardless of an approaching high note.

Gallwey states quite succinctly that, "People who really use their mind, free it from impeding their activity." This has been the important message throughout this book because it is at the core of the singing experience—both for the singer and for the audience. The great soprano Monserrat Caballe would seem to agree. She stated in the book *DIVA*, "From time to time in every artist's career [there are] moments when you no longer feel you're onstage making music, but in a different dimension, inside, at one with the music. The body is a concrete thing made up of physical matter. But when you are in this state of fusion with music, you are totally unaware of it. You feel light, weightless."

The term **inner game** is quite appropriate here. It is derived from Gallwey's belief that "every game is composed of two parts, an outer game and an inner game." The outer game is grounded in externals, while the inner game takes place in the mind of the performer. Technical training addresses the outer game, but it so often ignores the inner game which can aid or interfere with successful performances just as much as technical deficiency can. Many difficulties in performance are truly mental in origin. "We think too much about the elements of performance and try too hard to control movements. And we are too concerned about the results of our actions and how they might reflect on our self-image. In short, we worry too much and don't concentrate very well."

If our training involves the implementation of these principles of inner and outer preparation to begin with, the actual performing process will be a natural outgrowth and will lead a singer to an organic fulfillment of his or her potential. When performers sing correctly, they have food for concentration. When performers learn to sing with less than their potential, they absorb food for anxiety and tension. Recall the many references to tension and constriction mentioned in earlier chapters.

Referring to sources like Gallwey and Suzuki and Herrigel may seem like a case of strange bedfellows, but the concepts they elucidate are brilliant and absolutely applicable to the performance of singing on a higher plane. Musicians and athletes are alike in many ways. Both are performers who must spend time in repetitive training so that the appropriate muscle movements become smooth, efficient, free of constriction, and a matter of reflex.

As Gallwey states: "Quieting the mind means less thinking, calculating, judging, fearing, hoping, trying, regretting, controlling, jittering, or distracting; the mind is still when it is here and now in perfect oneness with the action and the actor." Like Nureyev at the apex of one of his leaps, a moment of suspension in mid-air, this point can only be achieved when the voice is truly a reflexive instrument creating whatever our desires ask of it.

It is every performer's goal: to be able to let go of the *doing process* and enjoy the *letting it happen process*. As Eugen Herrigel, author of *Zen in the Art of Archery* remarks:

> "How can the shot be losed if I do not do it?"
>
> "It shoots."
>
> "And who or what is this 'it'?"
>
> "Once you understand that, you will have no further need of me."

The "it" is *desire* coupled with reflex. This state can only be reached with a singing process that is built upon reflex—the **head voice**. We can produce the desired musical sound and can produce the moment of being "in the zone" if we have prepared and preserved our vocal instrument guided by our reflexes. And what an incredible experience to have this process guiding the voice, the most amazing musical instrument in the world.

Chapter 11
In the Final Analysis, Do You Deserve It?

Do You Deserve to Sing?

Many people with the desire to sing (as a hobby or for a career) stifle that impulse or give up on the pursuit for a wide variety of reasons. In my experience, for these people the predominant cause of this ambiguity, this sense of incompleteness boils down to this point: at heart, they think they just don't deserve to sing.

This feeling can take many forms. Add your own doubts and phobias to the list!

- Can I actually make a living doing this?
- Is music and singing a worthwhile endeavor?
- How can I expect someone else to support me while I go chasing moonbeams?
- If you are Pavarotti, it makes sense. But am I good enough for it to be worth while?
- Shouldn't I be at home with my family?
- Shouldn't I have a home and start a family?

Every fulfilling and artistic endeavor is open to this kind of self-doubt and scrutiny. Because of different childhood experiences, different machinations from this list may ring true with different people. It is interesting, though, that our culture's reward system pretty much guarantees that someone who loves to sing will question him or herself in at least one of these ways. How sad.

Music serves a basic and crucial function in human society.
Self-fulfillment is not the root of selfish.

The inherency of music in our lives and the desire to achieve a life-fulfilling goal are the two pillars supporting every singer's motivation. A singer recognizes both the profound value of music and the profound value of self-fulfillment. Against the world of self-doubt, serious professional competition, and sometimes scathing public criticism, these two pillars of motivation are a singer's foundation and support. These two basic, crucial, enormously meaningful concepts are the subject of centuries of discussion and shelves and shelves of books. The purpose of this chapter is to suggest that singers (novice or professional) should ask themselves one essential question:

Do I Deserve This?

Of course, whether we pursue and develop this activity that we love, or not has a profound impact on all other relationships as well. It's sad to see marriages and partnerships suffer because one person resents having to support the other person's dream. The antithesis is also true, though, that resentment can grow with time because a lost dream has been given up prematurely or under pressure. Putting off one's dreams equals putting off one's life and is the subject of the many facets of lost and found destiny.

Denying the dream unfortunately can work both ways. What a spouse or partner wants to be and do is part of who he or she is and what the other person fell in love with. By encouraging someone to fulfill a dream and realize his or her potential, we truly show how we feel about that person; we allow ourselves to become more a part of the other person's life. If one decides to change course concerning the dream or decides that he or she has invested as much in the pursuit of this career, adjusting will be easier. Both partners will have done their best by striving for the dream and by supporting the other; they now can accept the outcome without animosity. "I gave this all up for you" is not what anyone wants to hear. "Thanks for helping me pursue my dream" or "You helped me give it my best shot" helps a relationship survive and thrive.

Seeking realization of artistic potential in ourselves benefits our families, too. We show them strength, resolve, and the willingness to pursue meaningful goals, even if the goals are difficult to reach. Carefully understanding our dreams as adults also helps us avoid a basic parent trap: expecting one's child to give meaning to our lives. There are those parents for whom the child is made to accept a certain career choice as a way of fulfilling the dream of the parent. This route would undoubtedly lead to many years of therapy, resolving subconscious feelings of resentment. If a child or adult pursues his or her own dreams and goals, that person will be much happier.

Living by the principle that self-fulfillment is valid and valuable, we can find it easier to accept a partner's or our children's own career choices. It has become an often repeated truism that people who give themselves room to grow find it easier to give others room to grow also. This idea is mirrored in our actions so often because in real life the balance is hard to find; it is nonetheless worthwhile to try.

Many in their mid forties or fifties have walked into my studio wondering, "What could have been." I tell them that they do still have the right to continue the development of their singing voice. What will it mean in their lives at this point? The likelihood is that they will probably not go on to have any kind of career. But their lives will be enriched, and they will be happier through singing. Because of their singing, they can bring happiness to many other people's lives. Being able to sing in the local church choir is justification enough.

Years ago I recall one tenor who died on stage at the Metropolitan Opera during a performance. That in itself would be a grand and dramatic ending to one's career. But even more significant and noble for that musician was that he was sixty-three years old and had not begun that career until he was well into his forties. How wonderful it was that his age did not stop his pursuit. Most of us don't have the courage, strength, and conviction to start a second career at such an age or to struggle for many years without recognition.

Consider too that a singer is not like any other kind of musician. Pianists, violinists, flute players, percussionists, and all instrumentalists strive to find a sense of deep physical connection with their instruments. For vocal musicians, however, the physical connection is unique because the body is our instrument and the connection with that instrument is far more complete and intrinsic. This is the primal instrument our species has used to communicate feelings and emotions—moans, laughter, crying, screaming, singing. We have all communicated feelings in these ways. Although the profession may divide musicians in terms of our instruments, there is a singer in all of us.

Some people are able to connect their feelings with a musical mode of expression more strongly than others are. The stronger that physical connection is, quite often, the better a musician they become. They feel compelled to express themselves through this mode of communication. It's not fully understood why this happens, but this connection is very real and should be encouraged to its fullest. It enriches the lives of those who possess this drive; it enriches the lives of all those around these musicians.

The enrichment this connection gives is far more than just the benefit of pursuing self-fulfillment. I've said much about self-fulfillment, but have not even attempted to address the art itself. The artistic expression of human emotion accomplishes something of profound value to all of us. At the very least, that expression is a gift of effort and beauty given to the world with no strings attached. The devotion to one's potential to become a singer, poet, painter, sculptor, writer, musician, or artist of any kind is worth pursuing, even for a lifetime.

Do You Deserve to Sing Beautifully?

The fundamental purpose of this book has been to show that the pursuit of one's potential as a singer is the pursuit of a higher potential indeed. The beautiful, velvety voices of our culture's operatic past and present are not simply bizarre, unexplainable phenomena; the individuals from whose bodies those wondrous voices emanate are not Martians. The results we hear are because these performers sing in a particular way, using the vocal mechanism in a particular way. This particular way is the way of the **head voice**, and it is the way of singing that any of us can adopt as our way. It isn't the "lost art" of the great singers; it is an art that good and fine singers can use to change the quality of their sound and reach the aesthetic and ethereal pinnacle of the vocal art.

The **head voice** has now become a rare way of singing, a lost technique because it has been sidelined in our musical culture by "classical belting" and improper instruction, by the allure of musical theater, and by the failure to learn from the "great voices" who understood the "lost art" of the Golden Age of Voice. Three historical forces have played a part in this decline: changes in the popular musical styles we hear the most, an increase in the hyped up tempo and shrill of the modern sound, and the very far-reaching effects of the technology of amplification. As a result of these factors, most of us do not hear the **head voice** technique in singing as children in the daily experience of our popular culture. How can we even begin to produce something we experience so little?

The rarity of this way of singing is compounded by the fact that when a singer does discover the art of singing, he or she sounds so profoundly different from other singers out there. We assume that a singer is simply "a Martian"—somehow *other*, somehow not related to us and, therefore, not a realistic model for emulation. We think, "Well, of course, she (or he) is Leontyne, Birgit, Jussi, Joan,—far beyond my limited talents." This isn't the way it must be, though. We can change the current miserable state of singing if we look beyond the status quo. We must gather, listen, emulate, and teach the sounds of the past. We must look to the great singers through their recordings and live performances, through their books and master classes. We are not forced to accept the current state of the vocal profession; we can change if we seek change. We must seek that change through the real experts, the one's who have proven their worth and their integrity time and again on the opera stages and in the concert halls.

Simply accepting the current state of affairs in vocal music is the assumption I have wanted to challenge in this book. Opera singing has changed so much and not for the better. We are no longer living in the age of *Bel Canto*; we are unable to retreat further back in time to experience directly the era of Gregorian chant with its sounds floating through the splendid cathedrals. The velvety, ethereal sensibilities of singing in the **head voice** are slipping away in favor of the bark and bite of chest voice. There is in any age a group of singers who sing naturally in the head voice and rise above us mere mortals. They, in the hearts of the people, are granted name status and they are the ones to explain the attributes of the singing art. Don't assume that the exquisite velvety sound one hears from the special few voices is a gift of God, not given to ordinary singers.

It is a way of singing—one way of singing!

Pavarotti, when asked in an interview what made Pavarotti, "Pavarotti"—and no one else—he replied that everyday for two years his teacher made him work to place all the vowels in the same space and sensation as the closed Italian [u] vowel. When he finally accomplished this feat, and only then, did he become "Pavarotti." It took this amazing singer 400-600 lessons—if "everyday" was close to the truth—to discover his **head voice**. Our lesson from Pavarotti's experience is that we shouldn't give up on the dream!

Every voice that is **head voice dominant** is beautiful. The closer the singer comes to singing in this way, the closer he or she comes to the "greats." The singer soon realizes that this way of singing is attainable and available to anyone who is willing to commit. We, as an audience, hope that this will become, once again, the standard of the great operatic art form.

Reprinted from *The Wonderful O*, by James Thurber, and used with the permission of Simon and Schuster Publishers and Marc Simont, artist.

Chapter 12
The Learning Process and the Exercises

How to Start

The first step in learning to sing with the head voice is to develop the proper mind set. We are looking for a sound that we've not made yet, but we're in luck because we now have Mother Nature on our side. We're working within her domain and now realize that she is not a constrictive force. Our conscious mind can lead us down the wrong path sometimes, but Nature always gives us a barometer by which to measure rightness and correctness. That barometer is reflex and **sensation**. We can feel when we are tight and constricted and, therefore, can know when we are not singing correctly. Our job as a singer is to analyze what we hear and feel and experiment with ways to let go of the constriction and to accept freedom. We must tap into the right and surrender the wrong. Through our awareness and practice of the right **sensation**, we will know when we have reached the goal. With the correct feeling achieved through the head voice, the sound produced is our prize.

The prize will not come without effort, but in voice lessons or on our own time, we may often question whether we need a hundred "reps" of major and minor scales, of *appogitturas* and *staccatti* like push-ups and abdominal stretches at Gold's Gym. We may ask if we really need a thousand high notes covering the range of human hearing like exercises to strengthen our biceps and triceps and build our bulk. The answer is very simple— NO!

What then is the purpose of these exercises? How will they get us to the sound we seek? Quite a few teachers think that vocal exercises are for the purpose of stretching muscles to bring the voice to a certain type of music, or to create a certain type of voice. This thinking, this reasoning is absolutely wrong.

Repetitions and more practice represent a metaphysical change in **sensation** than actual development of vocal muscles. Proper practice helps us to understand and appreciate our barometer of sound and sensation; the various exercises we engage will help us develop and follow a path toward producing those sounds. We shouldn't mindlessly practice and repeat; we should understand, question, experiment, and discriminate. Once we find the path, it doesn't require a thousand tries if we are truly sensitive to what we are doing.

A Journey to Freedom

In my early twenties, I switched from *tenorino* to bass-baritone (this switch can be heard on the companion CD). A change that occurred because my voice teacher at the time had me exercising my voice low—at which point my voice fell into my chest-register and this booming sound came out (Caruso singing Colline!). So it was decided to push that to the top. This went on for 4 years—I stopped lessons and insisted that whatever sound I sang had to be easy and beautiful. I made these changes myself without the help of a teacher, and within 1 year had a lovely lyric-tenor voice, a first class voice (CD). Birgit Nilsson was the only person I ever worked with over a considerable period of time who corroborated my thoughts about vocal technique, shared her thoughts on the subject, and nurtured my own singing. What a fantastic person. She was a brilliant singer who at age 85 still was "as sharp as a tack" and could probably still put all of today's sopranos to shame with her high C.

So, back to the search to find the path to my lyric tenor voice: In 1975, when I was singing in the apprentice program of the Wolf Trap Company, I was covering the role of Michele in the Menotti opera *The Saint of Bleecker Street.* Michele sings the aria "*I know that you all hate me!*" which focuses on the word "home." "You foreigner, go back where you have come from; you foreigner, go back to your old home. My home, where is my home." The musical peak of the phrase occurs on 5th line F—on the word "home."

Polari

On a recording of this opera, David Polari, a wonderful young tenor who died in a plane crash at the beginning of his career, produced the most incredible sound on that 5th line F. I marveled jealously at the sound, but also wondered what he was doing to make that sound. I almost "stripped the gears" in my throat trying to replicate what I thought he was doing. I tried many times and many ways to produce that sound, but gained only frustration.

Bergonzi

(CD Track 10)

A few years later I had the opportunity to work with Carlo Bergonzi, the great international tenor. *[I had to keep my work with him "on the sly" because I was already taking lessons from a man regarded as one of New York's "finest" teachers, who claimed he was incorporating the head voice into my singing.]* At that time, though, I faced a serious dilemma in my voice and I was at a crossroads.

At Bergonzi's suggestion, we decided to work on the aria "*Io la vidi*" from Verdi's opera *Don Carlo*; he was singing it at the Met. In our work, he was trying to get me to sing a closed [u]. Many singers get caught up in the chest voice and all vowels become too open. And "too open" in essence means too much chest voice. I recall in one lesson Bergonzi became quite exasperated and exclaimed "No! [u]! [u]! [u]! Like in 'soon'!" Unfortunately, I produced [ao], thinking I was singing what he wanted. I could only produce an open [u].

Bergonzi also harangued me about the quality of my "O" vowel. He wanted a closed [o]; I could only produce an open [O]. The *Don Carlo* aria was filled with these two vowels and I was having a terrible time singing them closed as Bergonzi wished. He didn't give up on the importance of creating a closed vowel sound, but at that time in my vocal development I couldn't do it. I didn't really comprehend what he wanted from me. I didn't understand the importance of such an adjustment in my singing, but it was the beginning of my understanding, appreciation, and desire to sing in the head voice, to produce that exquisite sound I had heard earlier from David Polari. I was beginning to understand the importance of singing closed vowels; producing a closed vowel means singing it in the head voice. An open vowel adds more chest.

Kohn

I also was fortunate to have Eugene Kohn as my vocal coach. He helped me understand what Bergonzi wanted. He said that there was a beneficial texture in the [u] and that my voice sounded more beautiful when I used the [u].

Bergonzi could hear that my voice was in desperate need of *falsetto*, and he was using the [u] and [o] to influence the rest of the vowels. Kohn could hear the difference, also. My chest voice was so driven in my voice that it made these vowels impossible at the time. I realized that it was going to take some effort for me to rise to the next level in my development. This event was an epiphany for me and I began to rethink my singing. I knew that there was validity in what Bergonzi was saying, but it took me two more years to put the pieces together.

Meeting of the Minds

(CD Track 9)

I finally decided to bring these two "schools of voice" together and asked my voice teacher one day about the production of the closed vowels and the influence of their texture on the entire voice. I mentioned that Bergonzi emphasized a closed vowel sound. My voice teacher dismissed the concept claiming that Bergonzi didn't know what he was talking about and that this was why I was going to be the better singer. This response by my teacher shattered my image of him. "What I have?" I thought. He was referring to one of the world's great tenors who had a 40-year International career. His comment about Bergonzi altered my confidence. I had heard the perfect sound, but he was preaching otherwise. This was a sign from God. It was time to leave this teacher.

On my own I began working obsessively to develop that sound, the sound that consisted of closed vowels leading the way through the head voice. I discovered that [u] influences [o] and [o] influences [a]. As singers we should want the vowels to "feel" in a very small space: a small mouth position with pursed lips; an easy *mezzo-forte* to *mezzo-piano* dynamic in the initial learning, depending on the strength of the **head voice**; and stretching the vowels out into a spinning phrase. We should want the sounds to "feel" as though they are sitting on a cushion of air with no pressure and no push—just easy sound.

Pavarotti

My education in the **head voice** continued when I heard a BBC interview with Luciano Pavarotti; he was asked how he became "Pavarotti." His response was that his "entire technique is based on the closed Italian [u] which my first teacher drove into me for two long years. All the vowels must be in that same texture and feeling. After two years I got it and became 'Pavarotti.' " This broadcast confirmed what Bergonzi had been saying and what Christa Ludwig was asking of the students in that 1997 New York City Master Class when she asked "Where have all the head voices gone?"

Vowels and Quality of Sound

Three fantastic singers, three singers with fantastic careers couldn't be wrong. Gradually that [u] and [o] began to take shape in my voice, I started to see and appreciate music differently. Bellini, Donizetti, Puccini, Verdi, Menotti, and many other composers understood these vowels and used them, used them more than any other vowel in many cases. They understood that these vowels created a sound that was unusually beautiful although difficult to get to. When a singer "had" these vowels, he or she became an outstanding singer.

This was the key. The more I listened; the more I heard. The more I heard; the more I learned. How thrilling. This new view of singing and music was extremely exciting to me. I was becoming more sensitive and knowledgeable about that exquisite sound, and I was beginning to reproduce it with consistency.

This concept of the closed vowel with an easy dynamic to help achieve the head voice is the foundation of the correct sound. In practicing to achieve closed vowels, a student should become obsessed with producing that correct sound and the feeling. A student shouldn't worry at this point about the "weakness" of the sound; that will come with further development. The priority at this stage of the learning process is to reproduce the correct sound, that velvety, rich **head voice** texture in the sound, and to reproduce it consistently.

Tibetan Monks

One more character fashioned my understanding of vocal sound. Joseph Campbell, anthropologist and author of *The Universe*, wrote that when he was in Tibet working with the monks, they would sit all day and meditate—meditate while chanting the sound [om]. Campbell reported that when he asked about the genesis of this sound, he was told that [om] represented the entire universe and that it aligns the body both physically and mentally. The monks said that [om] begins with an [a], has an [o] as its core, and ends with a hum.

I wondered how they arrived at this understanding. This is certainly not the "AH" that coaches and conductors scream for to unknown students; this is different. It is the true Italian [a]. It is the [a] of Bergonzi and Pavarotti, of Ludwig and Nilsson, and now I had a fifth source, a universal source to confirm my understanding of vowel sounds.

Another point needs to be made here about the texture of the closed vowels. This vowel at the beginning of the conversion to a **head voice** sound will have a "wooly," maybe "hooty" texture. It may seem breathy initially, but it is the head voice. Those textures that are undesirable will fall by the wayside when the **head voice** element becomes more awakened. Remember Birgit Nilsson's teacher referring to her voice as sounding like a "foghorn," or a "steamboat coming down the river?" For four years she worked to get that sound out of her voice, but eventually realized that the "steamboat" was Birgit Nilsson. She was smart enough to understand that within that sound was what she was looking for—her **head voice**. But she said that it took her 10 years to get that negative sound out of her voice.

Obviously, the sound can't be left in that overly "wooly," "hooty" condition. But a student shouldn't feel frustrated about not producing that pure, rich, velvety **head voice** texture immediately. We shouldn't "throw out the baby with the bath water." With further work and attentive, discriminating listening, the desirable element in that initial sound, the seed of the **head voice** sound, will blossom.

Closed Vowels and the Head Voice

The closed [u] vowel contains the most **head voice**. If we match all the other vowels to it, we begin to realize that we aren't really referring to the vowel, but rather to a texture of sound that encompasses the entire vowel spectrum. This texture is created by using energy in an entirely different way. The energy feels "out front" and "in front of the lips." All the vowels begin to form themselves "out front." I've commented often that producing sound with the **head voice** produces no *sensation* in the body, especially in the throat The great singers refer only to the breath and the essence of their sound being "out front." So the only *sensation* in head voice singing with the rich velvety texture of sound is the use of the energy of singing in a different way.

A singer is constantly challenged to prevent that energy from dropping back into the throat. When it does, an experienced singer can immediately recognize that the sound will grab into the muscles and the texture will change.

All of the exercises used in the appendix to this book employ closed vowels. What exactly is meant by a closed vowel? In this context a closed vowel is one that is closed to the chest voice, but very open to the **head voice**. So if during the exercises a student feels that the sound is closing off, he or she needs to adjust and to persist in the drill; the most likely fault in this instance is that the chest voice is putting up a struggle to establish its dominance. When the chest voice finally surrenders this dominance, the student will feel the sound much higher and buoyant. The vowels will also sound strange because they are now of a different texture, a texture that is temporarily weak and will need strengthening. This adjustment occurs simply by finding that free spinning texture every time one sings.

Mirella Freni walked out of the hills of Modena (as Sutherland and many other great singers walked out of obscurity to operatic stardom) and sang [o] instead of [a]. Don't be intimidated by the "Ah God"; we have 63 different "AH" sounds in the English language and a singer needs to select the one that is most in the **head voice**, the one that is closest to [u] and [o].

What to Trust

G. B. Lamperti wrote, "Singing is a natural use of the voice. But to play on the larynx demands training of the brain and the body until desire and reflex control the process." To sing we need to consciously train our voices to play our musical instrument, the larynx, in a different way than we talk. It also means re-teaching ourselves how to sing in a different way. Lamperti calls it a "natural use of the voice," which means it must be free and unconstricted.

Essential Questions

I like this quotation from Lamperti; it establishes the fundamental problem of learning how to sing: *the union between desire and reflex*. One of the first questions I ask a new student is "*If you had access to your potential right now, how would you like to be able to sing?*" Almost every student agrees that he or she would like to have a full voice, rich and beautiful, easily produced with good top notes. Many also add they want their voices to express what they feel emotionally. These are descriptions of the **head voice**.

I also ask new students "*What kind of repertoire do you think you should be doing in an ideal situation?*" They almost always list the repertoire that I myself think they will be doing when their voices come into their own. It's amazing that the information about our voices is truly within us. It is the driving force behind our vocal study, our singing, and our self-image. If these three conditions are not part of a holistic union between body and mind, a singer will have a problem and will not achieve the level of the great singers.

In my pedagogy I like to establish the concept of discovery, discovery of a voice that is already there. Within the first lesson or two, I can always help a student to find and identify his or her **head voice**. The **head voice** of one student may be stronger than another's, depending on the degree of constriction the voice is accustomed to using. But every singer can generate and, therefore, discover it. When this discovery occurs, each student comments how effortless it is to produce the sound. Past experience often makes a student feel he or she should be "doing more" to produce such a rich sound and this thought needs to be eliminated. These students comment that they feel as if they should be tightening something, pushing something, holding, bracing, supporting, etc. It is amazing how much muscularity a singer will cope with before saying, "*Enough!*"

Many voice teachers instruct singing as though they were teaching weight lifting, requiring students to employ excessive muscularity along with a variety of contortions and gimmicks. By the time students feel that they are working too hard, they are probably quite beyond what their bodies can stand. Students may also notice high notes getting harder to reach or becoming non-existent. An erratic pulse may appear in the voice; a thickening of the sound may become apparent. A tendency toward illness will also increase—disease. Look at that word again: dis-ease, a lack of ease. How easy should it be to create beautiful singing?

"How easy do you want it to be?" The perception is that the great singers have had years of training and experience; therefore, singing is anything but easy. Their effort is perceived as talent and ability beyond our capabilities. The irony is that to sing like the great singers, regardless of training time and experience, should be a matter of being "easy," not unbelievable. That's the nature of the unconstricted, rich, velvety texture of the sound a great singer is able to produce by employing the **head voice**.

Tension in the Lips

Another issue worth discussion is the concept of "pursing the lips," which can be addressed in two ways. First, the shape of the mouth when singing is perhaps best explained by comparing it to the bell of a horn instrument. The bell helps direct the sound. With head voice singing, the sound is going to be pure and natural and the placement will be forward "out front." Direction is still necessary, hence the lips should be pursed without any tension; they should be formed as done in speech that is correctly produced. The lips are the steering wheel of the head voice.

There is another explanation of the "pursed lips" question. Without the head voice the mouth can hang loose and open and still purse without tension. The tension we'd feel will occur only when we start to make the sounds. The mouth will want to flatten out or spread to the side in response to the larynx rising. This, of course, depends on how much chest is contained in the sound because, as mentioned already, the degree of chest voice dictates the laryngeal movement. When the larynx moves up, it needs room. The muscles of the pharynx flatten out and the mouth follows suit. These two actions are combined. To create room for the larynx to rise, a chest voice trait, the mouth would have to be opened more. Singers will want to open wide going through the *passaggio*—upper E-flat to F#.

Singing in the **head voice** does not raise the larynx, and the lips will not want to flatten. Pursing the lips with a small mouth will create a condition that is not acceptable to the chest voice, and the head voice will be forced to perform the task. The key points: head voice technique; relaxed, but small lips; and a closed [u] vowel. These will produce an effortless and full sound with a rich and velvety texture.

Full Circle

Luciano Pavarotti has said that the mouth should be the size of a closed [u] vowel and that all the vowels are created in approximately the same space. This does not mean for a singer to "bite down on a pencil between the teeth," as is encouraged in some pedagogies. It means sing in the **head voice** which allows and encourages the mouth to be small. Pavarotti goes on to say that at first this mouth position can feel like taking the index finger of the right hand and maneuvering it through the fist of the left hand. A singer initially is not giving the voice the amount of space it is used to. The [u] vowel is [uuuuuuu . . .], not [o] and not a Texas [u], but an [u] that is full of *falsetto*. All the vowels must match this sensation.

Let's return to Menotti's opera *The Saint of Bleecker Street*, the lines of Michele, and the key word "home" or [om]. It is a sound that contains the most *falsetto* of all the vowels with the diphthong into [u] before the hum. The *falsetto*, the mechanism which when used freely does not raise the larynx, sounds other-worldly, incredibly facile, but incredibly beautiful. Consider and listen to Cecilia Bartoli, Karita Mattila, Kiri Te Kanawa, David Daniels, Anna Netrebko, and Ruth Ann Swenson. You'll hear that pure vowel sound with the *falsetto* mechanism. It is a sound that many great singers use in order to rush gingerly through runs or to pass boldly through the *passaggio* more easily, changing [a] to [o].

Notice the rest of the phrase from that "home" aria: "I do not want to belong, belong to this new world. I don't want to be told: you foreigners go back where you have come from! You foreigners, go back to your old home, my home, where is my home." Of these 39 words, we have 16 [o]'s, 8 [u]'s, 5 [om]'s, and 5 [w]'s that have [u] as the first split second or, in the case of "new," where the [u] is longer. It isn't a mystery that this phrase is so difficult for a singer, especially if he has a weak head voice. The aria becomes simply beautiful for any singer, though, with a strong **head voice**.

An exercise that I've used since the beginning of my **head voice** enlightenment is the phrase "YOU LOVE OUR HOME!" in various rhythmic patterns (Appendix & CD).

Unfortunately, not enough singers are learning to develop **head voice** technique. This is why Christa Ludwig, the great mezzo-soprano/soprano, commented after reading a draft of this book, how wonderful it was that I used the vowels "u" and "o" so often in my exercises (as have the great composers in their compositions). We singers need closed vowels and need to produce them in their pure form to show us the way "home."

In the fashion world there now exists the term "vanity sizes," meaning that the size listed on a garment is not the actual size. America, it seems, is getting fat but can't face the "music." So the fashion industry manufactures a larger garment, but labels it with a smaller size. Every customer then feels that he or she is in fact "ok" and has not gained weight. "No need to check on the scale because it is never correct!"

Vanity vs. Reality

In voice we have "vanity vowels." We think we are singing [o] and [u], but we really are not. That is why I had difficulty giving Carlo Bergonzi what he asked for. I was singing what I thought were the vowels. Most singers today aren't singing the correct vowels, the ones that the composer wanted. If we are to recover from the current predicament in voice, we must rediscover the lost art of singing. We must *produce vowels that belong to opera;* we must *employ the head voice.*

As an exercise, select any Shakespearian sonnet; pick your favorite. Read it as though you were a great British Shakespearian actor or actress. Go "over the top" with the reading. Think of the elocution of Eleanor Roosevelt, Richard Burton, and Julia Child. What are the vowels that they are using? Are they the everyday vowels we speak in conversations at the coffee shop? No! What you hear is the *Language of the Head Voice.*

In early television, great operatic singers would sing Broadway songs. Most listeners thought they were phonies. However, the following night, the same singer would be performing at the Metropolitan Opera—and the audience would stand, throw flowers, and applaud for 30 minutes. These singers were not singing differently; they were singing in the *Language of Opera—the Head Voice.* In recent times, this distinction has become considerably blurred. Many singers today are "crossover" performers delving into the realms of opera *and* musical theatre. Many, it seems, want to sing everything. Whereas the earlier singers couldn't "crossover," today's performer knows to use two different techniques—one with an unconstricted throat; the other with a constricted throat.

To maintain a high degree of integrity, opera must not succumb to a sound that lowers respect for the art. Opera is drama and music, requiring both melody and sound, to convey the meaning of the words. So, if we do not sing vowels with the proper sound quality—the words will not be what the composer wrote or intended. When we are able to access our **head voice**, all the vowels will change; they will become rounder; they will be more beautiful and much fuller with the pitch range that Mother Nature gave us. Our voice will finally take on the plushness and beauty of a great opera singer.

Hallel [uuuuu] ia!

In this book, elements of the **Head Voice** have been placed at your doorstep. You must take responsibility for your own voice. Don't surrender that responsibility to someone else; listen to the great singers of yesterday and today. Listen to what language they are singing in—their vowels and texture—and especially their u's and o's. Is it the language that you are singing in; is it the language of the head voice?

The Battle and the Balance

When the historical and incomparable soprano Jenny Lind was young, she lost her voice. After failing to regain it through prolonged study with Manuel Garcia in Paris, she went home, worked out the vocal problem herself, and became the greatest singer of her age. Birgit Nilsson early in her career was to sing Verdi's *Manzoni Requiem*. She caught a cold but didn't want to cancel because, as she said, she needed the money. She went into a practice room and came out several hours later having found her head voice and was now the "Birgit Nilsson" of record! Of course, the question always asked of her was "What did you do in that practice room?"

Epilogue

(CD Tracks 17, 18)

I've tried, through this book, to relay the journey of my own self-discovery of singing. It may have been at times an ordeal full of anguish, fear, and frustration, but ultimately the transcendence was a process that I needed to go through to discover what I now know about singing—singing like the great artists of the past. It is a journey I pass along to the next generation through teaching and through this book. Perhaps both experiences can make an impact upon the next generation. Perhaps the lost art can be reclaimed and quality singing can be recaptured and not remain lost.

You now have the tools to take into the practice room; you now can discover the voice that has been eluding you. So that your singing abilities can evolve into a talent, you must be willing to change and experience loss. Don't allow that surrender to frustrate you; the phoenix will rise out of the ashes of bad habits and wrong techniques if you have faith and confidence.

*Follow your mind and your heart—**Head First!***

THANK YOU

Exercises

1. A.

Repeat this exercise, descending in half steps down to E♭. Repeat the sequence many times, trying to establish a spinning, easy, relaxed, beautiful tone. Start with a dynamic of *mp*.

1. B.

2.

Using the relaxed, beautiful sound established in Ex. 1., continue the ease and dynamic into Ex. 2., bringing it down in half steps to C-G. Repeat this until you feel completely free of muscular interference

3.

Repeat with the same format as Ex. 2.

4.

Same format as Ex. 2. Always easy with *no* push.
Pursed lips, feeling the sound in front.

The feeling that one should try to establish on the [a] vowel is one that we get when we are sitting in front of the T.V. just about to fall asleep. The jaw falls open, and we could even start to drool. Totally relaxed!

Exercises 1-4 are the main exercises to repeat over and over, always trying to establish more ease and beauty. Easy easy easy! They can be used on all voice categories, modifying where necessary.

5. A.

5. B.

6.

The first note of each exercise is the most important. Think of it as the teacher. It will, if free, easy, and beautiful, teach the next notes to be the same. Always follow through with the exercises, just like you would in swinging a tennis racquet or golf club. Once the action starts, the energy continues through in the same direction to the end. Do not jump at the high notes. They are part of a legato phrase, and if the first note is sung correctly with a spinning, beautiful, soft-textured sound, the next notes will continue in the legato texture you have extablished.

7. A.

7. B.

8.

Sing exercises 7 and 8, continuing the texture of the initial [u] vowel. The sound will be felt in front of the lips, which will be slightly pursed.

9.

Always start at the top and bring the exercises *down* in half steps

10.

Appendix

8.7.88

Dear Denes,

Thank you very much for your kind greetings on my birthday. You made me very happy. I and my husband celebrated the day in Rome together with a few friends. I was afraid it would have gotten out of my hands if I would have stayed home. Still, I have to write a couple of hundred more "thank you" notes!!!!

I was so sorry that we did not get in touch any more after Delaware, when you saved my life! Thank You! I was waiting for Christine to call, because, as I said, I expected her to come to N.Y. and then we could have met all 3! She called at the very last minute, saying something else had come up, and she could not come. I had a letter from her last week. She was up in Canada appearing in a smaller role, and studying at the same time. She's loosing weight, she said. How are you? And the voice? Hope fine. I am wondering if something has come up concerning Europe?

Athis Tinnstal 8.7.88

Dear Dennis,

Thank you very much for your kind greetings on my birthday. You made me very happy.

I and my husband celebrated the day in Rome together with a few friends. I was afraid it would have gotten out of my hands if I would have stayed home. Still, I have to write a couple of hundred more thank-you notes!!!

I was so sorry that we did not get in touch any more, after Dresses, when you saved my life. Thank you!

I was waiting for Christine to call, because I expected her to cruise, as I said. I expected we could have come to N.Y. and then meet at 83. She called at the very last minute, before something else had come up, and she could not come. I had a letter from her last week. She was up in Canada, appearing in a musical hall and, singing at the same time. She said she's losing weight.

How are you? And the voice? Hope fine. I am wondering if something has come up concerning Europe?

I'll be in N.Y. November 12 - 22 and I'll be the Master of Ceremonies at the Richard Tucker Gala when the award will be given out, and I'll also teach at the Manhattan School again. Since I do not have quite that pressure, as when I was in N.Y. last time. I would like to listen to you, if you feel like, and if your time permits. I'll stay at the Mayflower Hotel again.

So far we had an unusual nice Summer, warm weather and lots of sun. I'll go to Bucheburg again this Autumn 8 – 23 of October. Well, I hope this finds you happy and healthy.

Hope to see you soon!

With all good wishes and much love,

Birgit

I'll be in N.Y. November 12–22 and
I'll be the Mistress of Ceremony at
the Richard Tucker Gala when the
award will be given out and I'll
also teach at the Manhattan School
again. Since I do not have quite
that pressure, as when I was in N.Y.
last time I would like to listen to
you, if you feel like and if your
time permits. I'll stay at the
Mayflower hotel again.

So far we had an unusual nice
Summer warm weather and lots
of sun. I'll go to Bückeburg
again this Autumn 8–23 of October.
Well, I hope this finds you happy
and healthy.

Hope to see you soon!

With all good wishes and much love

Birgit

1.5.89

Dear Denes,

Happy New Year! Thank you very much for your Christmas Card, the nice photo and for the cassette.

You sound really very good with lots of expression and fine pronunciation.

HOWEVER, I think what [that] you still are pressing the voice too much. Be more gentle! Let the voice get the intensity in your forehead and not so much in the throat. Relax! Try to take away the pressure. I know how difficult it is because you are trained that way, and it is hard to get the body, muscles and ear responding to it.

But I can hardly see how on your vocal cords . . .

Birgit Nilsson

Kristianstad 1-5-87

Dear Dawes,

Happy new year!

Thank you very much for your
Christmas card, the nice photo and
for the casett.
You found really very good
with lots of expressions and
fine pronunciations.
HOWEVER, I think what you
still over pressure the voice
too much. Be more gentle!
Let the voice get the intensity
in your forehead and not so
much in the throat. Relax! Try
to take away the pressure× I
know how difficult it is, because
you were trained that way, and it
is hard to get the body muscles
and ear responding to it.
But I can hardly see how

×on your vocal cords

you'll get through big roles without getting tired or hurting yourself, unless you have vocal cords of steel.

There are so many things which are better now, but the most important thing is not yet solved. As Lauritz Melchior said "one should sing on the interest and not on the capital."

I am glad that the audition in Chicago was a fruitful one. It was so nice seeing you and visiting with you in your lovely home.

We plan to go to Switzerland next week, where we also have a home. We have Spring here instead of Winter! Strange!

Forgive me for being hard on you. I think however it would do you lots of good if you completely could solve that pressure habit.

Lots of love,

Birgit

You'll get through big roles
without getting tired or hurting
yourself, unless you have
vocal cords of steal.

There are so many things which
are better now, but the most
important thing is not yet solved.
As Lauritz Melchior said, one should
sing on the interest and not on
the capital.

I am glad that the audition
in Chicago was a fruitful one
It was so nice seeing you and
visiting with you in your
lovely home.

We plan to go to Switzerland
next week, where we also have
a home. We have Spring here
instead of Winter! Strange!

Forgive me for being hard on
you. I think however it would do
you lots of good if you completely
could solve that pressure habit

Lots of love

Birgit

10.7.89

Dear Denes,

Thank you for your kind letter and the cassette.

Congratulations! You seem to be very busy. I am so glad that things are starting moving. You sound very good on the tape, much better than earlier. However—☺ I still think there is too much pressure on the voice. If you could eliminate that, it would be much easier to sing. Have you tried starting *pp cresc* to *ff* and back again with the voice at the same place and with not more pressure as that you use on *pp*. The <u>support</u> is doing the *crescendo* and not the throat. Well, so far you have achieved a lot. I only wish you to continue!

I was in Bucheburg this year again. It was beginning of September and the weather was . . .

Birgit Nilsson

Västrakarup 10.7.59

Dear Dennis,

Thank you for your kind letter and the cassette.

Congratulations! You seem to be very busy. I am so glad that during the [illegible] [illegible], you ~~sound~~ very good on the tape, much better than earlier. However, — ☺ I still think there is too much pressure on the voice. If you could eliminate that, it would be much easier to sing. Then you could [illegible] [illegible] [illegible] any [illegible] again with the force of the [illegible] [illegible] with not more pressure [illegible] [illegible] [illegible] [illegible]. The support is [illegible] the resonance and not the throat. [illegible] [illegible] [illegible] you have [illegible] a lot. I only wish you to continue!

I was in Bayreuth this year again. It was [illegible] [illegible] September and [illegible] [illegible] [illegible] so lovely. I work my period shorter, only 11 days. Last year had 16. But we cut off the concert [in the middle, which] always [was an unnecessary] one. So we had only a concert at the end.

I have also not heard from Christine since she won one of the Richard Tucker prizes last April. I also heard her at the Met. She sang lovely, but she was too "tame" for my taste. She has to get more "guts" or she'll remain as a church singer. I'll be in N.Y. November 5 – 13. The Met has invited me to "die Frau" on the 13th, and I'll be of course at the Manhattan School also.

I wish you loads of successes in Japan. I also hope you'll find nice half brothers and sisters in Houston. What an experience!!!

All the best and Much Love

Birgit

So [illegible]. I [illegible] ~~[illegible]~~ [illegible] [illegible] [illegible] [illegible] [illegible]. [illegible] [illegible] I had 16. But we [illegible] of the concert in the [illegible], [illegible] [illegible] [illegible] [illegible] [illegible]. So we had only a concert at the end.

I have also met [illegible] Christiansen ~~[illegible]~~ [illegible] one of [illegible] [illegible] [illegible] [illegible] [illegible] I [illegible] [illegible] in the [illegible]. She [illegible] [illegible] but she was the "Hanne" [illegible] [illegible]. She has to get [illegible] [illegible]. She'll remain as a church singer. [illegible] November 5–13. The [illegible] will be in the "[illegible] FRAU" [illegible] [illegible] [illegible] the 13th [illegible] [illegible] [illegible] [illegible] Schubert [illegible].

I wish you lots of success in Japan. Also hope you'll find nice half brothers and sisters in Houston. What an experience!!

All the best and much love

[illegible]

12-27-90

Dear Denes,

First of all I want to wish you a happy and successful New Year! I am just back from Switzerland where we spent the Christmas.

Thanks for the cassette. I think it is marvelous!! Congratulations, you sound very good. As it is now I think the Italian roles suit you very well. That little "extra pressure," which you still have, goes fine with the Italian repertoire—you have really progressed! I am glad! You seem to be busy with difficult obligations which is wonderful.

Hope Ariadne goes fine. The tenor part is difficult and high. Give Christine my love.

We have no snow here in South Sweden. But in Switzerland was lots of snow.

Much love,

Birgit

[illegible] 12.27.90

Dear Doris,

First of all I want to wish you a happy and successful new year. I am just back from Switzerland where we spent the Christmas.

Thanks for the cassette. I think it is marvelous! Congratulations. Your sound very good. As it is there, I think the Italian Arias suite you very well. That little "extra pressure" which you sometimes have, goes fine with the Italian repertoire – you have really progressed. I am glad you seem to be busy with different obligations which is wonderful. Hope Aida goes fine. The tessitura is difficult and high. Give Christine my love.

We have no snow here in South Sweden. But in Switz. we had lots of snow.

Much love

Birgit

Dear Denes,

WOW!!! I had just finished your X-card [Christmas] when the big parcel arrived, full of excellent news and other goodies. Thank you very much.

Well, first of all, Congratulations! It's absolutely fantastic that you have been able, alone, to put this Festival together. I do not know for anything in the world how you did it. You must be one of the seventh, or at least eighth Wonder. I am so glad for you! Hurrah! Hojotoho!!!

I have not listened to the cassette yet, because I have to have a bit more time and quiet. I am in a bit of hurry now.

Dear Dames
Wow!!! I had just finished
your X-card when the big
parcel arrived, full of excellent
news and other goodies. Thank you
very much.
Well, first of all, Congratulations!
It's absolutely fantastic that
you have been able, alone,
to put this festival together
I do not know for anything in
the world how you did it.
You must be one of the seven, or
at least eight wonders. I am so glad
for you! Hurrah! Hojotoho!!!
I have not listened to the cassette yet,
because I have to have a bit more time
and quiet. I am in a bit of
hurry now.

→

Sorry about all the sad things which recently happened to you!

I was thinking so much of you the 11th of September, hoping that you were not in that terrible catastrophe. I did not sleep for a whole week. How little we know what can happen the next minute?

Take Care. Have a rest now. Congratulations again!

Much love

Birgit

Sorry about all the bad
things which recently happened
to you!
I was thinking so much of
you the 11th of September,
hoping that you were not in
that terribel catastrophy.
I did not sleep for a whole
week. ~~How little~~ we know
what can happen the next
minute?
Take care. Have a nice time
Congratulations again!
Much Love
Bil

February 6, 02

Dear Denes

I am so sorry My X-mas Card came back yesterday. I wrote the wrong [number]. In my old book is written 825. But in my new book was 823. Sorry, Sorry!

In the meantime I have of course been listening to the Walkure, and I am very impressed. I can not understand how you did it! The singers are very good. I liked the Wotan too. He seemed to have more experience.

A big fan of mine, whom I hardly know, is making an exhibition of all the things he has collected during 50 years about me. It's in [Malcion]. He has 32 . . .

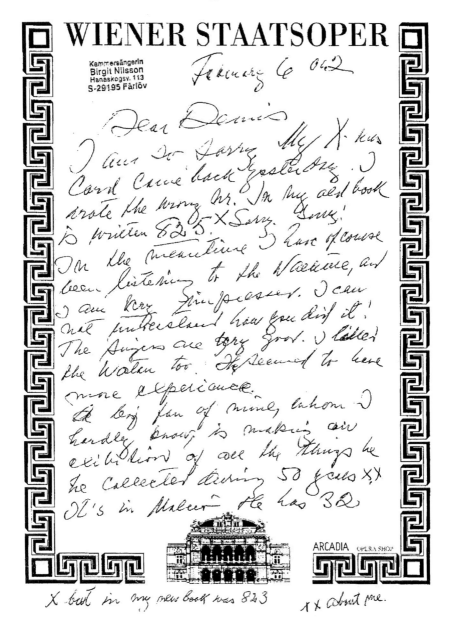

WIENER STAATSOPER

Kammersängerin
Birgit Nilsson
Hanaskogsv. 113
S-29195 Fårlöv

February 6 002

Dear Dennis
I am so sorry. My X-mas
Card came back yesterday. I
wrote the wrong Nr. In my old book
is written 825. X Sorry Sorry!
In the meantime I have of course
been listening to the Walküre, and
I am very impressed. I can
not understand how you did it!
The singers are very good. I liked
the Walan too. He seemed to have
more experience.
A big fan of mine, whom I
hardly know, is making an
exibition of all the things he
he collected during 50 years XX
It's in Malmö. He has 32

ARCADIA OPERA SHOP

X but in my new book was 823 XX about me.

Scrapbooks, programs, posters, etc., etc. It is absolutely marvelous. I borrowed him 4 costumes and some costume jewelries. Well, one never stops to be surprised.

I have just come back from Stockholm where I was giving a lecture at the Royal Musical Academy on Saturday. I'll be in Gottenburg where they will give the whole Walkure in concert version. I'll make a speech before and tell the public what [it] is all about. They are having very good singers, Alesandra Marc, Brünhilda, and Nina Stemme (last years Senta at the Met) Siegleinda.

Forgive me for my big mistake concerning the address and congratulations once more!!!

Love,

Birgit

Scrapbooks, programs, posters
etc. etc. It is absolutely
marvelous. I borrowed him
4 costumes and some costume jewelries.
~~well~~ Well, one never stops to be
surprised.
I have just come back from
Stockholm where I was giving
a lecture at the Royal Musical
Academy. On Saturday I'll
be in Gothenburg where they will
give the whole Walküre in concert-
version. I'll make a speech before
and tell the public what is all about.
They are having very good singers
Alexandra Marc, Brünnhilde and Nina
Stemme (last years Senta at the Met)
Sieglinde.
Forgive me for my big mistake
concerning the address and congratulations once more!!!

Love
Birgit

November 8th 02

Dear Denes,

I was soooo glad to receive your package and your letter today!

As you see from my earlier letter, I lost your new address, and I was very upset and unhappy.

Thank you so very much for the CD's and the programs today. At the moment I have no possibility to listen because we are going to Stockholm where I am giving a masterclass and thereafter we are going to Las Palmas in Gran Canaria where I'll give a speech at a Wagner-Congress. Normally I am not all that busy. It is just now it's coming at the same time. I have not been feeling well lately because of bad pains in my hip. Luckily I have found a medicine which has helped me a lot (NO DRUGS!) and I am very happy for that.

I can not tell how impressed I am with your work. So far I have been looking at the programs and reading your letter. <u>How</u> on the earth are you doing it? You must have a sixth sense. I am so . . .

November 8th 02

Birgit Nilsson

Dear Doris,

I was soooo glad to receive your package and your letter today!
As you see from my earlier letter, I lost your new adress, and I was very upset and unhappy.
Thank you so very much for the CD:s and the program today. At the moment I have no possibility to listen because we are going to Stockholm where I am giving a masterclass and thereafter we are going to Las Palmas in Gran Canaria where I'll give a speech at a Wagner-congress. Naturally I am not all that busy, it is just now it's coming at the same time. I have not been feeling well lately because of bad pains in my hip. Luckily I have found a medicin which has helped me a lot (NO DRUGS!) and I am very happy for that.
I can not see how impressed I am with your work. So far I have been looking at the program and reading your letter. How on the earth are you doing it? You must have a sixth sense. I am so

happy for you that everything works so well for you. But please, do not overdo it!!! The burden of the work seems inhuman to me.

I have to have this letter sent to you as fast as possible. You'll hear from me again when I have been listening to your CD's.

Congratulations to your success and succeeding!!!

All the best, and much love

♥ Birgit

happy for you that everything
works so well for you. But please,
do not overdo it!!! The [illegible]
of the work seems phenomenal to
me.
I want to have this letter sent
to you as fast as possible. You'll
hear from me again when I have
been listening to your C.D.'s.
Congratulations to your success
and succeeding!!!
all the best, and much love
Birgit

My dear Denes,

All my best wishes for a jolly good Christmas and a successful 2003. ♥

Birgit

God Jul & Gott Nytt År

Best Wishes for a
Happy Christmas
and
a Wonderful New Year.
Love
Birgit "*con Sordino*"

Best wishes for a
happy Christmas
and
a wonderful New Year.
Love
Birgit "con Bordino"

Index

15 Rah Exercise *37*
abdomen *14, 16, 17, 82*
acoustical facts *7*
acoustics *25*
  dead halls *34*
acting out *23*
actor *44, 45, 87, 104*
adrenaline *48*
aesthetic *8, 56, 92*
Aida 63, 73
air flow *42*
Albany Symphony Orchestra *v*
alcohol *39, 48*
Aler, John *6*
Alexander Technique *45*
Alexander, F.M. *45*
allergies *41*
amplified music *28, 30*
amplitude *5*
Annaheim, Ellwood *xv*
anxiety *46, 47*
anxiety-begetting *50*
Arabella 35
Ariadne auf Naxos viii, 27
Arroyo, Martina *viii*
articulate meaning *26*
asthma *41*
Atlanta Opera *70*
audition committees *33*
auditions *47*
aural beauty *26, 27*
authority figures *49*
bad habits *19, 82, 105*
B-adrinoceptor antagonists *48*
Balkema, John *xv*
barking *33, 44, 72*
Bartoli, Cecilia *103*
Battle, Kathleen *31, 32, 69*
Bayreuth *iv, 70*
BBC *98*
Bel Canto *vii, 53, 55, 57, 58, 93*
Bell Laboratories *56*
Bennett, Rodney Russell *52*
Bergonzi, Carlo *viii, 97, 98, 99, 103*
beta-blockers *48*
Bjoerling, Jussi *xvii, 9, 19, 48, 63, 72, 73, 77*
blood flow *42*
body use *44*
bracing *4, 6, 16, 17, 18, 21, 22, 30, 101*
brain *19, 45, 48, 85, 100*
breath *xi, xiii, 13, 15, 16, 17, 18, 19, 20, 22, 30, 34, 49, 75, 76, 78, 79, 81, 82, 100*
  sustaining *22*
breathing *vii, 13, 16, 18, 22, 44*
  correct *13, 14*
Brightman, Sarah *viii*
Broadway *32, 61, 104*
Buckaburg, Germany *iv*
Burch, Bruce *iii, xv*
Burton, Richard *104*
Caballe, Monserrat *xvii, 6, 19, 27, 55, 71, 72, 75, 86*
Calabi, Marcella *xv*
Callas, Maria *8, 44, 55*
Campbell, Joseph *99*
Carerras, Jose *59*
Carey, Mariah *28*
Carmen 70
Carmina Burana 6
Caruso, Enrico *15, 96*
Cavaradossi *70*
CD *viii, ix, xiii, 3, 67, 68, 70, 82, 96, 97, 98, 103, 105*
chemical waste *42*
chest voice *3, 5, 6, 7, 8, 9, 13, 16, 18, 20, 21, 24, 28, 30, 32, 33,*

34, 37, 39, 42, 44, 45, 57, 60, 61, 62, 66, 71, 74, 75, 78, 83, 93, 97, 100, 102
Child, Julia *7, 22, 28, 104*
choke *xviii, 17, 47, 49, 62*
chronic conditions *41*
clarity *25, 28*
clown *44*
coaches *xix, 26, 27, 33, 83, 99*
colds and viruses *41*
Columbia Artists Management *68*
conductors *viii, xix, 33, 99*
confidence *v, 33, 41, 49, 50, 67, 85, 98, 105*
  lack of *46*
consonants *6, 30*
constriction *vii, xviii, 7, 15, 16, 17, 18, 19, 20, 24, 25, 27, 30, 31, 37, 39, 41, 43, 44, 45, 56, 60, 62, 66, 72, 75, 87, 95, 101*
contortion *25, 42*
Cordovana, Michael *iii, xv, 69*
Corelli, Franco *iii, xiii, 6, 9, 53, 55, 73*
Cossotto, Fiorenza *xvii, 9*
coughing *41*
cricoids *24*
crossover *8, 29, 71, 104*
cultural norms *19*
Dallas Opera *viii, 59, 67, 68*
dancer *44, 77*
Daniels, David *63, 103*
deception *50*
Dellacote, Jacque *viii*
depression 48, 66
Der Ring des Nibelungen 73
di Stephano, Giuseppe *62*
diaphragm *15, 16, 21, 47*
Diaz, Justino *viii*
diction *26, 27, 28, 58*
Dictionary of Vocal Terminology 83
Die Meistersinger von Nürnberg iii, viii, 69, 70
Die Walküre iv, v, viii
Dimitrova, Ghena *5*
dis-ease *51*
disorientation *48*
Don Carlo viii, 71, 97
Don Jose *70*
dynamics *31*
ear, human *7, 56*
easefulness *51*
Ed Sullivan Show, The iii, 69
ego-mind *86*
elocution *7, 28, 104*
Emerson, Ralph Waldo *10*
emotion *xix, 26, 29, 32, 33, 38, 91*
environment *17, 21, 50, 83*
Escamillo *66*
EST *39*
Ewing, Maria *viii, 70*
exercises *15, 29, 38, 95, 96, 100, 103*
exhalation *13*
expression *xviii, 7, 26, 27, 30, 91*
falsetto *6, 7, 17, 24, 57, 60, 61, 63, 74, 76, 77, 83, 84, 97, 103*
falsetto-dominated registration *57*
  full-voiced falsetto *63*
Farrell, Eileen *8*
Faust 65
feel, mental health *46*
Feldenkrais *45*
Festspiele Haus *iv*
Figaro *66*
finishing school *7*
first rehearsals *47*
Fisk, June *70*
Fitzgerald, Ella *28*
Flack, Roberta *28*
Flagstadt, Kirsten *48*
  Met debut of *56*
Flanigan, Lauren *51, 58, 71*
Fleming, Renee *71*
fluidity *29, 30*
frame of mind *86*

freedom *3, 8, 10, 15, 19, 26, 30, 35, 38, 44, 60, 62, 63, 78, 81, 85, 95*
Freni, Mirella *29, 55, 100*
frequencies *7, 24, 32, 33, 48, 56, 75*
singer's frequency *56*
friction *42, 43*
full-voiced *xvii, 7*
Gallwey, W. Timothy *85, 86, 87*
Garcia, Manuel *10, 58, 105*
Gauci, Miriam *viii*
Gencer, Leyla *viii*
gestures *23, 30, 31, 44*
Ghiarov, Nicolai *xiii*
Gianni Schicci *66*
gift, the *81*
Glass, Philip *52*
Golden Age *7, 28, 71, 72, 83, 92*
Golden Age of Singing *7, 28*
Goldovsky Opera *viii, 67*
Götterdämmerung v
Great Singers on Great Singing 55
Gregorian chant *93*
habits, ingrained *44*
Harrell, Mack *32*
head texture *7*
head voice *i, iii, v, vii, viii, ix, xvii, xviii, xix, 3, 4, 5, 6, 7, 8, 9, 11, 13, 17, 18, 19, 20, 21, 22, 24, 25, 26, 28, 29, 30, 31, 32, 33, 34, 35, 37, 38, 39, 42, 43, 44, 45, 46, 50, 51, 52, 55, 56, 58, 60, 61, 62, 63, 65, 66, 67, 69, 70, 71, 72, 73, 74, 75, 76, 78, 81, 82, 85, 86, 87, 92, 93, 95, 97, 98, 99, 100, 101, 102, 103, 104, 105*
health *20, 38, 41, 42, 43, 44, 45, 46, 51*
hearing *xvii, 9, 13, 25, 26, 28, 29, 95*
heart beat, rapid *48*
heldentenor *5*
Herrigel, Eugen *86, 87*
high blood *48*
high notes *9, 17, 24, 25, 28, 30, 60, 73, 76, 81, 95, 101*
Hines, Jerome *55*
holistic union *101*
hooty texture *99*
Horowitz, Vladimir *49*
hyoid bone *81*
hyperactive airways *41*
hypnosis *39*
I Lombardi 58
I Puritani 68, 73
illusions *50*
inarticulate meaning *26, 27*
inhalation *13, 16, 21*
Innaurato, Albert *73*
Inner Game of Tennis, The 85
integrity *50, 82, 92, 104*
intensity *13, 32, 69*
internal monologue *50*
intuition *79*
Io la vidi 97
irritability *46*
Italian Method of Singing *78*
italianate *29, 73*
Janacek, Leos *37*
jaw *15, 83*
jazz *8, 28*
Kohn, Eugene *viii, 97*
Koussevitsky Arts Center *v*
Krause, Alfredo *59*
La Boheme viii, 67
La Fanciulla del West viii, 70
La Perichole viii
La Rondine 62
Doretta's aria *62*
Lamperti, G. B. *78, 100, 101*
Language of Opera—the Head Voice 104
laryngeal manipulation *4*
laryngoscope *10, 58, 76*
larynx *xi, xiii, 6, 7, 8, 15, 16, 17, 18, 19, 22, 23, 24, 25, 39, 42,*

56, 57, 60, 61, 62, 66, 74, 75, 81, 82, 100, 102, 103
legato *22, 28, 30, 58*
letting go *34, 51*
Levine, James *58*
Lind, Jenny *105*
Linz Philharmonic *52*
lips, pursing *102*
Lucrezia Borgia 59
Ludwig, Christa *ix, xiii, xvii, 9, 98, 99, 103*
lyric soprano *5, 9, 51*
Macropoulos Case, The 37
Madama Butterfly viii
magic formula *15*
Maltz, Maxwell *39*
Manahan, George *viii*
Mancini, Giovanni *82*
Manzoni Requiem 105
Marton, Eva *5*
master class *iii, iv, xvii, 69, 75, 76, 98*
Mattila, Karita *9, 71, 103*
mega-rock concerts *38*
Melchior, Lauritz *48*
Merman, Ethel *7*
Merrill, Robert *xiii, xvii, 8, 55, 73, 82*
Metropolitan Opera Competition *66, 67*
Metropolitan Opera Guild Office *iii*
Metropolitan Opera *iii, xviii, 7, 27, 35, 47, 56, 58, 66, 67, 68, 71, 91, 97, 104*
microphones *71*
Midgette, Anne *1, 83*
Milanov, Zinka *xvii, 75, 77*
Minnesota Opera *70*
Moffo, Anna *8*
Montreal International Vocal Competition *66*
Mother Nature *31, 95, 104*
motion *29, 75*
mouth *15, 23, 24, 60, 75, 83, 98, 102*
muscles *xviii, 10, 11, 14, 15, 18, 20, 21, 22, 24, 39, 47, 57, 60, 62, 73, 74, 75, 77, 78, 81, 83, 86, 95, 96, 100, 102*
    chest muscles *66, 75*
    intercostal muscles *15*
    knotted muscles *44*
    muscle power *9*
musical theater *28, 29, 32, 65, 92*
musicality *vii, 23, 29, 30*
musicianship *29, 30, 31*
Music-Minus-One *viii*
Myer, Edmund J. *57*
natural flow *18*
natural phenomenon *10, 58*
nerves *46*
Netherlands Opera *67*
Netrebko, Anna *8, 103*
neurosis *48*
New York Times, The 1, 83
Nilsson, Birgit *iii, iv, v, vii, viii, ix, xi, xiii, xvii, 5, 21, 22, 32, 44, 63, 69, 70, 71, 82, 92, 96, 99, 105*
    Nilsson's *Electra 56*
nonverbal messages *27*
Norma viii, 70
O sole mio xviii, 73
opening nights *47*
open-throated *8*
Opera News 71, 73, 74
Opera North *70*
Opera Theater *71*
operatic career *48*
orchestral rehearsals *47*
Ordonez, Antonio *viii*
Otello viii
overtones *24, 25, 26, 28*
Pape, Rene *xiii*
parents *49, 51, 80, 90*
passaggio *59, 60, 62, 63, 84, 102, 103*

Pavarotti, Luciano *xiii, xvii, xviii, 9, 29, 55, 58, 59, 62, 63, 72, 82, 89, 93, 98, 99, 102*
pedagogies *9, 102*
pharmaceutical companies *48*
pharynx *xi, 23, 42, 60, 77, 102*
philosophy *86*
phlegm *42, 43*
physical health *41, 44*
pianissimo *6, 25, 71, 73, 75, 81*
pitch *6, 7, 13, 17, 23, 24, 25, 26, 32, 37, 38, 60, 74, 75, 83, 104*
  pitch range *7, 24, 104*
placement *xi, 7, 55, 60, 62, 102*
Polari, David *96, 97*
Pollione *70*
Ponselle, Rosa *55, 77*
potential *v, xviii, 9, 19, 48, 70, 85, 86, 87, 90, 92, 101*
Practical Reflections on Figured Singing *82*
prescribed drugs *48*
pressure *16, 17, 18, 20, 21, 24, 25, 30, 34, 42, 43, 47, 48, 56, 61, 62, 75, 90, 98*
pressurized sound *45*
Price, Leontyne *xiii, xvii, 8, 51, 55, 66, 72, 73, 75, 76, 81, 82*
Providence Opera *viii*
psychiatrists *48*
Psychocybernetics *39*
quality *viii, 5, 7, 17, 20, 21, 22, 26, 27, 28, 33, 34, 45, 50, 51, 58, 62, 66, 68, 69, 71, 72, 73, 74, 75, 77, 78, 82, 85, 92, 97, 104, 105*
reflex *78, 85, 86, 87, 95, 100, 101*
reflexive self *51, 85*
reflux *41*
regional finalist *66*
registers *3, 4, 5, 6, 7, 8, 24, 26, 57, 59, 60, 61, 62, 66, 74, 83, 84, 96*
rehearsal schedule *41*
Reid, Cornelius *83*
relaxation *13, 14*
repertoire *xix, 9, 32, 34, 35, 51, 69, 80, 101*
Rescigno, Nicola *viii*
resonance *15, 34, 52, 56, 60, 81*
respiratory *xiii, 16, 23, 24, 39, 41, 42, 43, 44, 46, 75, 76*
rest *xvii, 3, 18, 20, 21, 27, 55, 62, 67, 73, 78, 81, 97, 103*
restlessness *44*
Riedel, Debra *viii*
rock gods *38*
rock-radio *38*
roles, heavier *34*
Roosevelt, Eleanor *7, 22, 28, 37, 104*
Rostropovich, Mstislav *viii*
Saint of Bleecker Street, The viii, *96, 103*
Santa Fe Opera *9*
Sataloff and Robert, *48*
scamming *50*
Scotto, Renata *8*
self-abuse *48*
self-image *33, 87, 101*
self-medication *48*
self-worth *33*
Shaker Mountain Opera *v*
Shakespeare, William *29*
short-term memory loss *48*
shouting *xviii, 71, 74*
shrill *27, 44, 76, 83, 92*
Siegfried iv, *70*
Siegmund *iv*
Sills, Beverly *viii, 34*
Sinatra, Frank *28*
singing,
  great *15*
  insecure *49*
  labored *44*
  professional *7*
sinus trouble *41*
sitzprobes *47*

Smith, Malcolm *viii*
soft palate *15, 23, 42, 81*
sound production *20, 25, 26, 44*
speaking voice *xiii, 7, 37, 38*
speech *xviii, xix, 7, 8, 27, 28, 29, 37, 38, 48, 74, 102*
spinning out *25, 29, 34*
spread *23, 24, 84, 102*
stage fright *48, 49*
stage presence *44*
Stagefright: How It Can Work for You 47
Stanley, Douglas *9*
Stockholm Conservatory *21*
Strasberg, Lee *38*
stress *46, 48*
stressors *46*
Striny, Denes *v, viii, ix, xv, 70*
suffocating *16*
support *xi, 5, 63, 77, 79, 89, 90*
Sutherland, Joan *xiii, xvii, 4, 8, 10, 19, 22, 31, 32, 55, 72, 73, 82, 100*
Suzuki, D. T. *86, 87*
Swenson, Ruth Ann *xiii, 9, 32, 71, 103*
synthesizers *71*
tai chi *45*
Tanglewood *6*
Te Kanawa, Kiri *xvii, 4, 9, 10, 35, 103*
teachers *vii, viii, xiii, xvii, 3, 4, 5, 6, 10, 9, 13, 14, 18, 21, 28, 30, 37, 45, 47, 49, 52, 57, 58, 59, 66, 67, 68, 70, 71,72,73, 74, 75, 76, 77, 78, 79, 80, 81, 82, 83, 85, 93, 95, 96, 97, 98, 99, 101*
Tebaldi, Renata *8, 70*
technical skill *10*
technique *viii, 4, 8, 10, 14, 19, 21, 25, 26, 27, 28, 31, 38, 42, 43, 45, 49, 51, 55, 56, 61, 63, 66, 70, 72, 73, 76, 78, 80, 83, 86, 92, 96, 98, 102, 103*
tenorino *3, 65, 96*
tension *iii, xix, 10, 15, 16, 17, 18, 19, 20, 21, 23, 24, 25, 27, 34, 39, 42, 44, 45, 46, 47, 48, 49, 50, 81, 87, 102*
terminology *xiii, 77*
tessitura *62*
Tetrazzini, Luisa *78*
text *vii, 23, 26*
words *26, 29*
texture *xiii, 15*
The Art of Singing 78
therapists *48*
therapy *48, 49, 91*
thoracic *16*
throat doctors *48*
throat, too open *60, 62, 97*
throaty *4, 10, 38, 44, 58, 72, 81, 83*
Tibetan monks *99*
tickle *42*
tone of voice *27*
Torna surriento 38
Tosca 68
training *xix, 10, 19, 50, 55, 69, 80, 86, 87, 100, 101*
tranquilizers *48*
Traviata, Lisbon *56*
tremor *48*
Trinity College *67*
Triplett, Robert *47*
Troyanos, Tatiana *viii*
trust *10, 26, 33, 34, 49, 70, 84, 85*
Tucker, Richard *55, 72, 73*
tuning fork *75*
Turandot iii, viii, 56, 69, 73
Turandot, Rio *56*
Universe, The 99
valve *xiii, 13, 16, 17, 18, 19, 20*
vanity sizes *103*
vibration *23, 24, 75*
Virginia Opera *70*
visualization *23*

vocal
    vocal cords *xi, 16, 24, 42, 43, 48*
    vocal exercises *95*
    vocal holes *61*
    vocal production *10*
    vocal self-image *vii, 37*
voice
    voice, beautiful *5, 15, 68*
    voice, belt *8, 61*
    voice, big *5, 32, 33*
    voice, big enough *31, 33*
    voice, building *77*
    voice, carrying power *vii, 23, 31, 28, 32, 33, 34*
    voice category *4, 39*
    voice, mixed *8*
    voice students *xv, 10, 25*
    voice teacherism *81*
    voice, unconstricted *xviii, 39*
volume *31*
vowel spectrum *100*
vowels *7, 9, 28, 30, 34, 53, 62, 63, 76, 79, 81, 93, 97, 98, 99, 100, 102, 103, 104*
    vowels, closed *100*
    vowels, vanity *103*
Wagner soprano *34*
Wagner, Wieland *iv, 44*
Wagner, Wolfgang *70*
Walther *iii, 69, 70*
Warren, Leonard *xvii, 9, 73*
Washington Opera, The *viii, 67*
Watanabe, Yoko *viii*
Wintersturmme viii
Wolf Trap Co. *viii, 67, 96*
yoga *45*
Zen in the Art of Archery 86, 87
zen-like *34*
zone, getting in *34, 51, 85, 86, 87*